Perfect Phrases™ for Presenting Business Strategies

Perfect Phrases™ for Presenting Business Strategies

**Hundreds of Ready-to-Use
Phrases for Writing Effective,
Informative, and Powerful
Strategy Presentations**

Don Debelak

New York Chicago San Francisco Lisbon
London Madrid Mexico City Milan New Delhi
San Juan Seoul Singapore Sydney Toronto

The **McGraw·Hill** *Companies*

Copyright © 2010 by The McGraw-Hill Companies, Inc. All rights reserved. Printed in the United States of America. Except as permitted under the United States Copyright Act of 1976, no part of this publication may be reproduced or distributed in any form or by any means, or stored in a database or retrieval system, without the prior written permission of the publisher.

1 2 3 4 5 6 7 8 9 0   FGR/FGR   0 1 0 9

ISBN: 978-0-07-163996-5
MHID: 0-07-163996-9

This book is printed on acid-free paper.

McGraw-Hill books are available at special quantity discounts to use as premiums and sales promotions, or for use in corporate training programs. To contact a representative please e-mail us at bulk-sales@mcgraw-hill.com.

Contents

Contents

Chapter 11 Making Money   125

External Strategies   126
Internal Strategies   131

Part Three: Closing Out: Getting Commitments   137

Chapter 12 Explain the Key Tasks   139

External Strategies   140
Internal Strategies   145

Chapter 13 Detail the Advantages   151

External Strategies   152
Internal Strategies   155

Chapter 14 Ask for Action   161

External Strategies   162
Internal Strategies   165

Part Four: Sample Presentations   171

Chapter 15 Sample Presentations— External Strategies   173

Presentation to Management—Create a
    Competitive Advantage   173
Presentation to Action-Oriented People—
    Solve a Problem   178

Contents

Chapter 16 Sample Presentations— Internal Strategies 195

Introduction

People in business present varying strategies for changing a company's operations, anywhere from creating a new way to processing intercompany memos to deciding on a new marketing strategy. Almost all decisions in a business are typically a result of someone presenting a strategy that is eventually adopted. People present strategies all the time and their success within the company depends on their ability to have these strategies accepted. For example, a company might decide, based on a determination by top management, to implement a strategy of lean manufacturing throughout all departments in order to cut costs and eliminate as much outsourcing as possible. That would be a decision with major impact on the organization because of the potential efficiency gains, the amount of resources needed, and the management time required to implement the strategy. But in fact, successful implementation of that initial strategy requires probably hundreds of smaller operational strategies. Some of those operational strategies need to address questions like these:

- How should purchasing ensure materials arrive just in time?
- How can each department be arranged to smooth production?

- What is the best plant software package to use?
- How should each production area be reorganized for lean manufacturing?

There are often dozens of issues to address regarding how to implement almost any decision in a company. How are those decisions made? Someone presents a strategy that is eventually accepted. My goal in writing this book is to help readers present strategies that have a major impact on their organization, and to guide them through the entire process of implementation. I believe your ability to have your strategies turn into decisions will position you as a leader or future leader in your organization.

The Book's Format

Three Major Sections

The book starts with a section on making people comfortable, delivering the strategy in a context that people relate to and that doesn't rock the boat too much. While you are excited about your strategy, most people are going to receive your message with skepticism. The perfect counter to that skepticism is to make people relax and see you are delivering a strategy they can live with. The second section covers how then to deliver the message with power. In the end, all companies need to constantly reinvent themselves to move forward in a rapidly changing world, and they have to be concerned about changing to fit their new environment, growing their sales, and most importantly making money. You can't do that while feeling comfortable. This section is what top management wants to hear more than any other, and it is also the section that scares most employees. But most people will be able to accept your strategy if you've done your job right making people comfortable. The third section deals with closing the deal, getting commitments from people to accept your strategy. You may not get a full commitment to start, but you want to at least maintain a commitment that will keep your strategy alive. The last two chapters of the book offer examples of strategy presentations to help readers understand the entire presentation process.

External and Internal Strategies

Each chapter has two parts—external and internal strategies. External strategies, which deal with markets, customers, and vendors, typically have a positive impact on the entire organization, either on profitability or revenue, and call for a straightforward approach. Presenting an internal strategy must be done diplomatically as most, if not all, strategies adversely impact someone in the organization or are opposed by others with competing strategies. As a result, internal strategies often need to be presented in a way that doesn't upset too many people.

Many strategies have both external and internal components, for example, cutting lead time by 50 percent is a strategy that has external benefits—customers will appreciate quicker delivery. But the implementation falls mostly on operations, people in production, and production control. Whenever a strategy's implementation falls on operations people it should be considered an internal strategy. The strategy can be considered external when the implementation is by top management or sales and marketing or others who primarily work with external contacts.

Purpose of the Strategies

The internal and external parts of the chapter are then divided into four sections that are based on four common purposes of strategies:

- Solving a problem
- Improving performance
- Creating a strategic advantage
- Addressing new opportunities

I've found these four categories cover virtually every strategy. Look at all the phrases for all four purposes before selecting one to be sure you pick the phrase that will sell best to your audience.

Outlook of Person Evaluating the Presentation

Knowing which perfect phrase for all presentations depends on your audience. Each type of person requires a different approach in order to convince them to move forward. Four perfect phrases are presented for each strategy purpose, one for each of these different types of people:

- Higher management
- Action-oriented
- Analytical
- Conservative or resistant to the strategy

Again, be sure to look at all examples before zeroing in on the phrase you will use, especially when presenting to multiple people who may have different outlooks.

Each chapter then offers 32 perfect phrases, 16 for external strategies and 16 for internal strategies. As an example, the first four phrases listed in the external section of the chapter will be:

- Purpose: Solving a Problem/Audience: Higher Management
- Purpose: Solving a Problem/Audience: Action-Oriented
- Purpose: Solving a Problem/Audience: Analytical
- Purpose: Solving a Problem/Audience: Conservative or Resistant

Try to Emphasize External Strategies

Most people will present far fewer external business strategies than they do internal strategies. But I've found trying to focus on creating external strategies offers many benefits. First, they are the strategies that produce what companies value the most: higher revenues, profits, and market share. Internal strategies are often focused more on costs. Second, external strategies also provide the best opportunity for recognition as presenters find it easier to hold onto ownership of a strategy, especially if the strategy is presented on paper or in a group setting. Internal business strategies are frequently discussed by many players and often employees, especially employees in middle management and down, find their ownership of the strategy co-opted by more senior management.

Presenting to an Audience of People with Varied Outlooks

There may be times when you are presenting to people that are members of all four groups: higher management, action-oriented, analytical, and conservative. Or you will present to a group with two or three types of people. I found that it works best to try to include a statement for each type of person present. It will stretch out your presentation, but my experience is that people tend only to hear the message targeted at them, and the presentation will go much more smoothly when they feel it relates to their specific goals.

Adaptations

The perfect phrases in this book are examples of the type of phrase you should be using on every point. You will need to adapt these phrases to the actual strategies and situations you are addressing. I've included sample strategy presentations in the last two chapters of the book so you can see how these adaptations will actually occur.

Perfect Phrases™ for Presenting Business Strategies

Part One

Making Listeners Comfortable

People listen to most new strategies with skepticism unless you are the top manager, and in many cases even if you are the top manager. They are ready to chop down your ideas either because they fear change, have their ideas to promote, or are just comfortable with how the business is currently running. There is no point starting out on the defensive with listeners looking to find weaknesses in your strategy which they can exploit. So instead, start out making every effort to assure the listeners that your strategy will fit right in with the corporate goals and organization and that you are providing a strategy that they can accept and adopt, showing progress on their part without changing their world too much. Your company or your position in the company is going to decay, of course, if all your strategies fit into "making people comfortable." But taking the strategy up a notch to where it can change the business comes in Part Two, Delivering the Power. First, you must put your listeners in a receptive mood.

Chapter 1

Craft the Opening Statement

The job of the opening statement is to first catch the attention of your audience and to encourage the listener to be receptive to your strategy. The best way to produce that result is to make a statement that reflects what the audience wants or needs to hear when it is presented with a new strategy. You'll get off to a fast start by crafting your opening statement with phrases that address what the audience wants to hear.

All of the phrases listed in this and in subsequent chapters start with the word *I*. Be sure to use the word *we* instead if the strategy is created by the team.

External Strategies

External strategies, which reflect on the operations of the company that impact outside organizations—typically a company's distribution network, investors, or customers—often have a major impact on a company's sales and bottom line. Most companies look for new external strategies all the time. But they are also cautious because a company can only create a major new external strategy occasionally and management will be concerned that if a new strategy doesn't produce a positive impact it will create a negative perception in the market. So you need to expect people to listen, but also expect them to be careful.

Solving a Problem

Higher management wants to hear: Enhances the company in the market.

I've created a strategy that will produce kudos for us in the market while eliminating the (state what the problem is) problem we are facing today.

Action-oriented wants to hear: Solution will be implemented quickly.

I've come up with a solution to the (problem name) that we can introduce within four weeks.

Analytical wants to hear: Benefit justifies the cost.

I believe we can address the (problem name) cost-effectively. I've analyzed the costs and believe that we have one strategy available that satisfies the customer without hurting our bottom line.

Conservative or hostile needs to hear: Strategy is risk-free and provides strong motivation to move ahead.

The (problem name) may escalate and cause us some serious bottom-line damage. I've come up with one solution that is low cost and risk-free that we can implement without causing too much turmoil in the organization.

Improving Performance

Higher management wants to hear: More profit, higher market share; and better customer service.

I've created a strategy that provides the total solution that customers have told us they want that will position us as the market's preferred provider, which will generate higher profits and market share.

Action-oriented wants to hear: A quick introduction to generate momentum.

I believe I've discovered a strategy that will energize both the sales force and the plant to the high levels we have seen in periods where the company had peak performance.

Analytical wants to hear: Cost benefit analysis.

Over the last three weeks I've been analyzing a cost-effective strategy that offers the customers and prospects the increased performance they want.

Conservative or hostile needs to hear: You are avoiding a risk.

The company has been looking for a way to increase our customers' perception of our products' performance. I believe I have developed a strategy to do that with minimum risk.

Creating a Strategic Advantage

Higher management wants to hear: Positioned to be a market leader.

A corporate goal over the past year has been to create a strategic market advantage. I have a strategy that creates an advantage that I believe will result in our being perceived as the market leader.

Action-oriented wants to hear: Create momentum in the marketplace.

I know many people are looking to reenergize the staff. This new strategy should do just that as it gives the company a strong competitive advantage that will be quickly perceived both internally and externally.

Analytical wants to hear: Risks and rewards.

Bold strategies are exciting but they often come with risks. I have a proposed strategy where I've been weighing the risk-reward ratios and I find it creates a strategic advantage with only minor risks.

Conservative or hostile needs to hear: Company needs to avoid falling behind by standing still.

The company's best days occurred when it had a strong strategic advantage. Without that advantage our position has slipped. I have a new proposal that not only will stop our market slide, but put us back on top.

Addressing New Opportunities

Higher management wants to hear: Strengthen the brand; increase market share.

Many in the company have recognized the new opportunity (state the opportunity). I've developed a strategy that can capitalize on this major upside potential while strengthening our brand and increasing our overall market share.

Action-oriented wants to hear: Move quickly.

Our competitors must be seeing the new opportunity (state the opportunity) as well as we are. I have a strategy in mind that will let us move proactively into the market with a response before anyone else.

Analytical wants to hear: Carefully thought out.

The new opportunity (state the opportunity) has everyone considering new ideas. Rather than rush the idea in front of people, I've spent the past few weeks evaluating it to be sure we have an approach our competitors can't top.

Conservative or hostile needs to hear: Risk of inaction is high.

There are risks in addressing this new opportunity (state the opportunity) but failing to act could pull down our bottom line for several years. I have a proposed strategy that lets us act in a major way but minimizes risk.

Internal Strategies

Presenting internal strategies is more difficult than presenting external strategies. First, they typically aren't as glamorous as external strategies, and second, an internal strategy often impacts many others in the organization who may not want to make any changes. You need to use great care to present an internal strategy without any gaps in your thought process or the strategy is almost certain to be rejected.

Solving a Problem

Higher management wants to hear: More profit, better quality, and less required resources.

Company management has stated they want to cut our overhead burden as a percent of revenue. I've done a study and feel I have a strategy that will not just meet your goal, but exceed it by 25 percent.

Action-oriented wants to hear: Solution implemented quickly.

We have faced the problem of (state what the problem is) for over six months without any resolution. I've come up with a solution that we can introduce within four weeks and implement with a team of just three members.

Analytical wants to hear: Benefit justifies the problem of change.

The (state the problem) needs to be resolved. If we can do that we will be back on track to hit our budgeted profitability, but we need to find a solution people can buy into so they will be willing to change. I've been talking about my proposed strategy to several groups and they all feel it will meet our corporate cost goals.

Conservative or hostile needs to hear: Risk-free with strong motivation to move ahead.

The problem of (state the problem) has caught management's attention and I have the sense they are frustrated because nothing has been done to date. I have a solution that I feel will show management we aren't dragging our heels and I feel we can implement with only minor adjustments to what we are doing now.

Improving Performance

Higher management wants to hear: More profit; better image; increased market share.

My strategy will cut our lead time by 50 percent. That will cut manufacturing costs as well as produce substantial external benefits including increasing our market share over competitor X.

Action-oriented wants to hear: Fast implementation; increased morale.

This approach calls for just a few changes in our production assignments and will expedite movement through the plant, as well as cut scrap. The decreased costs should motivate plant people as they will hit their budgeted cost reduction targets sooner.

Analytical wants to hear: Cost benefit analysis.

Sales management believes a shorter lead time strategy driven by the new production system will increase sales 20 percent. Maintaining lower inventory levels will also cut our overhead burden 10 to 20 percent. Those benefits will pay for the changes in four months.

Conservative or hostile needs to hear: You are avoiding a risk.

We need to look at changing our production system to cut lead time as our competition has been reducing their lead time and we run the risk of losing sales. My proposed strategy will keep us ahead of competition while cutting our costs without disrupting our current manufacturing processes.

Creating a Strategic Advantage

Higher management wants to hear: Enhances the company in the market.

The strategy I'm proposing will leapfrog the major changes our competitors have made over the last two years. We can guarantee we have the right product specialist available for projects to ensure we complete jobs on time.

Action-oriented wants to hear: Strategy can be implemented in a short timeframe without major problems.

I've developed a strategy that can quickly change our technical service response team's customer service ratings and as a result give us a strategic advantage over every competitor in the market.

Analytical wants to hear: Benefit justifies the cost.

Our current production utilizes over 95 percent unique parts for each product line. I believe a strategy that will standardize as many production parts as possible could cut our cost. I did an analysis of two of our five major selling products and feel that we can cut costs 18 percent. We would have a nine-month payback period to cover our reengineering costs.

Conservative or hostile needs to hear: Risk-free with strong motivation to move ahead.

We haven't changed our IT staffing or procedures for five years despite many technological changes and constant reorganizations at most other companies. Studies in the industry have shown one strategy (state the strategy's name) cuts costs and improves performance. If we make the change I'm proposing the risks will be small as the strategy has already been tested at dozens of other companies.

Addressing New Opportunities

New internal opportunities revolve typically around the use of new technology, implementing new practices and procedures that have been developed by other organizations or another part of the organization, restructuring, or implementing processes or procedures requested by customers or prospects.

Higher management wants to hear: Enhances the company's progressive image; better profitability.

The company has worked hard to have the image as the most progressive company in the field. We can enhance that image and lower our warranty costs if we implement some of the new quality procedures that have been adopted by our major customers.

Action-oriented wants to hear: Taking advantage of the new opportunity will build momentum and not drag down the company with implementation delays.

The new strategy for streamlining new product introductions that I'm proposing can result in increasing momentum in the market. I believe we can have a smooth implementation by having a three-person task force prepare an action plan that will provide a smooth transition.

Analytical wants to hear: Benefit justifies the cost.

The reorganization I'm proposing will cut our costs and reduce our outsourcing needs. The other side of the question of risks and implementation costs: I've studied the benefits and costs and feel this strategy will have a very strong benefit to cost ratio.

Conservative or hostile needs to hear: The proposed change is overdue; not moving will leave the organization behind competitors.

The department hasn't changed staffing levels for over four years, despite technology changes. The department may have just expanded work to keep the staff busy. I have a proposed reorganization that will allow us to ensure we are only doing the work required. This will help the company address the pricing pressure we are facing.

Chapter 2

Show Careful Consideration

Y ou walk a fine line in making a strategy presentation. If you don't provide lead-in comments to your strategy you won't give listeners a framework on how they should respond. For example, consider a strategy that improves a company's customer service department so it will position you as a market leader over the next three years. Without preliminary comments that set the stage a listener might feel you are trying to solve a current problem and respond that your solution is overkill. On the other hand, people will be irritated if you take too long to present your strategy. So your comments must be brief and to the point in your introductions. Both the opening statements and statements that show you have taken careful consideration should take no more than 60 to 90 seconds. Any longer than that and your audience might turn against you.

External Strategies

People often present strategies without thinking through all of the ramifications and considerations of their choices. You need to quickly demonstrate that this isn't the case with you. You can show your consideration by stating in some way you have eval-uated the idea by: examining similar introductions from others, conducting research with others outside your company, or through discussions and evaluations from others within the company. You can also do an independent evaluation without using any outside sources, but typically you will run into resist-ance, especially on an external strategy as people will be wary if you don't have any support from others.

Solving a Problem

Higher management wants to hear: Strategy has worked; risk is small.

Our top two distributors both reported that two other companies (name the companies) have used the same strategy I'll be proposing to successfully address the problem. Since those companies responded, both have increased market share.

Action-oriented wants to hear: Solution is easy for all to understand and implement.

According to our regional directors, two other companies implemented the strategy I'll be explaining with a team of six and they had area-wide implementation within four weeks.

Analytical wants to hear: The chances of success are high based on others' experience.

I'm going to recommend a strategy that has been used successfully in our market five times, without a failure, according to what I have learned at industry meetings.

Conservative or hostile needs to hear: Strategy is a proven winner; the risks of not moving forward are high.

Our company has used the same procedures for five years before this problem developed. The problem has developed because our customers have changed while we haven't. We will only get in more trouble if we don't offer a solution, and I'm able to show you several examples of how my proposed strategy has worked in the past.

Improving Performance

Higher management wants to hear: Program will move ahead without any issues; strategy will increase the bottom line.

I've found three examples of where other companies have introduced the strategy I'm presenting. All three have significant increases in their margins and all three implemented the strategy with only minor difficulties.

Action-oriented wants to hear: Strategy will be noticed both internally and externally; strategy can be quickly implemented.

While the company is always looking for low-risk performance improvements, this is a particularly good time to move ahead as we haven't had many improvements in our operations the last few years and the strategy I'll be discussing is one everyone will notice.

Analytical wants to hear: Cost benefit analysis experienced by others.

I decided to present the following strategy after talking to three industry consultants at the last trade show. They all confirmed a payback ratio of anywhere from 3 to 1 to 5 to 1 in savings over program costs in the first year of implementation.

Conservative or hostile needs to hear: The risk is in not moving forward; the strategy can be implemented without problems.

The strategy I'm proposing has been effective in improving other companies' performance, but I know there will be resistance to moving ahead. But in this case I believe the real risk to the company is standing still. Our industry is adapting, and we need to adapt along with it.

Creating a Strategic Advantage

Higher management wants to hear: Huge upside with minimal risks; potential results verified by others.

I've researched the strategy I'll be proposing in two other product areas that serve our market. In both cases the implementing company's market share grew by five points within two years.

Action-oriented wants to hear: Others have succeeded; success can be easily duplicated.

A similar strategy to my proposal was introduced originally three years ago by a company in a related industry, and I've located two other companies who have introduced this strategy in the last year to achieve a strategic advantage. All reports indicate these introductions were trouble-free.

Analytical wants to hear: Result of others in similar situations who have implemented the strategy.

We can only periodically implement a strategy for strategic advantage. It is important that we ensure we can succeed. I've looked at three industries similar to ours and found several companies that have succeeded with similar strategies.

Conservative or hostile needs to hear: Company needs to avoid falling behind by standing still; success is likely.

The strategy I will propose has already been adopted with success in similar markets and has been freely discussed in the industry media. I believe we need to move quickly before our competition does.

Addressing New Opportunities

Higher management wants to hear: Opportunity has a high probability of significant increases in sales and market share.

This strategy addresses a new opportunity due to technology shifts. Several industries have seen this shift earlier in their industries than we have. Companies in those industries employing a similar strategy to the one I'm proposing have produced sales gains of 15 to 25 percent.

Action-oriented wants to hear: Opportunity can be exploited quickly with little internal turmoil.

This opportunity has come up in company conversations for the last few months. Based on other companies' success, the strategy I'm proposing can be implemented in less than three months.

Analytical wants to hear: Upside probabilities trump downside risks.

The company evaluates new opportunities as they develop, but I'm recommending moving ahead with this strategy as all reports show strong upside for companies that have followed this approach.

Conservative or hostile needs to hear: Risk of inaction is high.

The opportunity I'd like to address with my proposal is bigger than any we've seen in the last few years. If we pass on this, we may regret it for years while we wait for the next opportunity to come around again.

Internal Strategies

External strategies are easier to justify because often information is readily available about how other companies have implemented the strategy. Successful internal strategies also get media coverage, or at least discussion, at conferences and industry events. But companies can and do try to keep internal strategies secret while external strategies are easily observed by the market. If you can't give concrete examples of other companies' success, concentrate instead on how others in the organization support your strategy. To get the input you need to generate initial support for your strategy you will need to share the strategy with others while it is still in its development stage. You can do this without a full strategy presentation by prefacing your remarks to others with the comment that you have "an idea you are kicking around and you feel it is important to get some feedback from people who have first-hand experience with the situation."

Solving a Problem

Higher management wants to hear: Others agree that this is the right approach.

I realize that a strategy for solving problems only works when it has strong internal support. I've checked with the four key people who will be involved in implementation and they all support the strategy in its concept stage.

Action-oriented wants to hear: Others have implemented similar solutions without any major problems.

I've researched trade magazines in other industries for other companies that have implemented similar strategies and I have found three contacts who all believe the strategy I'm proposing will quickly solve our problem.

Analytical wants to hear: The problem will be solved cost effectively.

The three contacts I've located at other companies that have successfully implemented this strategy all claim the costs were quickly recouped by solving the problem.

Conservative or hostile needs to hear: High probability of success; potentially bad consequences for those who resist.

Top management has been unhappy about this problem and wants a solution. The strategy I'm proposing is one that people in the company support and that has been successfully used in other companies.

Improving Performance

Higher management wants to hear: Increased profitability; implementing solution won't distract from other efforts.

My proposal is for a strategy that has been highlighted at a recent trade conference due to its success at other companies and it meets the company objective of raising margins 1 to 2 percent per year.

Action-oriented wants to hear: Strategy will be successful and accepted by others; will build momentum.

Improving our performance in the (state department or operation where performance will be improved) is identified as a key company goal. The approach I'll suggest meets that goal, has already been accepted by others in the corporation, and can be implemented quickly.

Analytical wants to hear: Cost benefit analysis.

The strategy I'm proposing should have a payback period of less than nine months if our results are similar to the case study presentations I have heard at trade association meetings.

Conservative or hostile needs to hear: The risks of not implementing the strategy are greater than the risk of moving forward.

Our processes in the (state the name) department have not changed in four years while our competitors have each twice improved their processes and cut their costs. In one other market the company that failed to implement this strategy ended up at a competitive disadvantage

because its lead time was 50 percent more than its
competition's.

Creating a Strategic Advantage

Higher management wants to hear: Enhances the
company's progressive image; motivational for the
employees.

Another company in a related industry released a report
after implementing this strategy. In that report the company
discussed how overall company morale rose as employees
considered the strategy an exciting development.

Action-oriented wants to hear: Wide support for program.

I've discussed the strategy with several managers after a
presentation at a local industry event. They all felt the
strategy had potential and merited a look.

Analytical wants to hear: Proven strong benefits to justify
costs and risks.

The strategy I'm proposing will give us a much quicker
response to potential production problems. I have
received cost proposals from three consultants and all
project a monthly cost that is 30 percent our current
scrap rate.

Conservative or hostile need to hear: Benefits are proven
and so strong they can't be overlooked.

Eighty percent of the affected managers support
investigating this type of strategy because it will allow the
company to exceed all its department objectives. The
resulting lower costs will give us a strategic advantage on

large automotive contracts. We have no other proposals active that produce even half the benefits of this strategy.

Addressing New Opportunities

Higher management wants to hear: Strategy has strong internal support or has been proven to provide significant benefits.

This strategy has been studied by several managers at recent industry conferences, and all believe implementing the new production ordering will cut our production time by 25 percent.

Action-oriented wants to hear: Successful implementation without internal resistance.

My strategy is a slight modification of a strategy already implemented at our Wilkes-Barre, Pennsylvania branch. That plan has been effective and we can introduce and debug it within six months.

Analytical wants to hear: Likely success with a result that is worth the effort.

I recognize we have limited resources to exploit opportunities that improve the operations in the (state name) department. But this strategy has been used by many major companies, greatly improving their operations, and now new technology makes it a viable strategy for companies of our size.

Conservative or hostile needs to hear: The expected success is assured; the company will weaken its competitive position by not acting.

Making Listeners Comfortable

The strategy I'm presenting has worked for enough companies that we know it can succeed, and if we choose to outsource implementation there is a network of consultants that we can hire. What is more important is that our department's margins have been eroding and we need to move our profitability back up to keep corporate support for our new projects.

Chapter 3

Introduce the Strategy

This chapter deals with introducing the strategy as an overview. You should be able to summarize your strategy in just two or three sentences that everyone can understand.

External Strategies

Companies have several issues they consider with external strategies. First, a poor decision for a policy with major impact will be remembered by customers and prospects for a long time. Second, management worries the market will consider them conservative, lacking innovation, and not being customer friendly if the company doesn't introduce new external strategies. Finally, changes in external strategies can have a big impact on market share and sales revenue. You can expect people to always be interested in a new external strategy, but they will be skeptical as they will fear failure. I've used one proposed strategy for each type of situation. For example, in the Solving a Problem section, the statement of strategy is the same for each type of person you present to, but your immediate follow-up comment after describing the strategy will vary depending on the person you are talking to. Each section of the chapter lists the statement of the situation and the proposed strategy first, and then the follow-up comments appropriate to your listeners' outlook.

Solving a Problem

The description of the situation and statement of strategy are:

> We've lost three distributors in the Southeast and our customers aren't getting the service they need. Reliant Technologies is a regional company in the Southeast that makes a complementary product that it distributes through its direct sales force. Reliant is willing to handle distribution of our product through their sales force and I recommend we pursue that strategy.

Higher management wants to hear: Strategy will be more that an "it's about time solution" but instead be perceived as a positive step forward.

> Reliant has a strong reputation and market presence that will give customers and prospects confidence that we are dramatically increasing our customer support in the Southeast market. The program should be effective as Reliant stands to gain as much as we do. They will have access to our customers to whom they are not currently selling, and adding our line will cut down their sales and marketing cost percentage to the industry average.

Action-oriented wants to hear: Solution can be easily and quickly implemented.

One third of Reliant's sales reps have previously worked with one of our former distributors. Going with Reliant will be a much shorter route to establishing a firm Southeast U.S. presence than trying to line up and train new distributors.

Analytical wants to hear: The strategy makes sense financially and the program has been carefully researched.

Our promotional, training, and consignment costs will be 30 to 50 percent less than if we were to attempt to develop a new network of distributors. I've talked to Reliant's sales manager and 30 percent of its sales staff, and they are projecting sales that will be two to three times the sales levels of our distributors in their peak years. I've also spoken with the service staff. They are well qualified and in several cases already experienced with our products.

Conservative or hostile needs to hear: We must move ahead and this is the best choice.

We have no choice but to create a solution since the Southeast is a major part of our market. The two other proposed options include finding new distributors and setting up our own sales force, which is either too uncertain or too expensive. Using Reliant is the only strategy that moves ahead quickly with minimum risk and costs.

Improving Performance

The description of the situation and statement of strategy are:

Our customer base for our IT services has many small companies where many employees work at home or on the road. These professionals often work offline from their servers and there is a risk of their data being lost unless they have a system to regularly back up both the data on the server and on individual computers. I'm proposing we add a new service that backs up all of a company's computers three times a week.

Higher management wants to hear: Significant impact in the market, noticeable impact on profits and market share.

Our niche market consists of small companies with a high percentage of professionals. We need to increase our service level to keep our position as the leading technology provider for this market. Adding a comprehensive backup service will increase sales to current customers, help add new customers, and keep us ahead of competition.

Action-oriented wants to hear: Strategy will be noticed both internally and externally and strategy can be quickly implemented.

I've talked to our technology manager and he feels we can set up and equip three-worker teams that can implement the backup system from our offices within 48 hours of a customer signing up. The teams can be ready to go in four weeks and we can coordinate a large e-mail marketing campaign when the team is ready.

Analytical wants to hear: Decision has been studied carefully, margins and market acceptance have been considered.

I've discussed this strategy with our service group manager and four of our customers. Our service manager feels that once a customer is set up the costs of continuing backup will be minimal and we will price the service with a 75 percent margin. I've discussed this with several customers, and they all feel the service is desired if we can customize it to meet their needs rather than offering a standard package.

Conservative or hostile needs to hear: The risk is in not moving forward.

Our revenue per customer has been dropping, primarily because we have improved the reliability of our customers' networks and software. To make up the revenue shortfall we need to both increase our number of customers and also find additional services to maintain revenue from existing customers.

Creating a Strategic Advantage

The description of the situation and proposed strategy are:

Our malleable *dental crowns* and new products for taking impressions have been recognized by dentists as the best option for seniors, as it minimizes the chances of creating new cracks in the tooth. My proposal is to turn this into a strategic advantage by forming a senior patient division, creating an advisory board of crown and bridge specialists and an alliance with leading dental schools to further improve our current line and develop new products for seniors.

Higher management wants to hear: Large upside with minimal risks.

The number of crowns is increasing over 10 percent per year, primarily because of the increase in dental work on seniors. No other manufacturer has developed products specifically for that market. Experts in senior care are anxious to have the ear of a major company to create needed products. We should also expect a strong line of senior products to help other products in the line. Our risks are small as our dental advisors will be willing to promote the products they helped design.

Action-oriented wants to hear: Program can be implemented quickly and the market advantage we create will be strong.

Currently there are no "senior friendly" products on the market. We have had inquiries and support from dentists who concentrate on elderly patients for senior-oriented products. We just need to align part of the resources in the R&D group to work with our new group of advisors to execute this strategy.

Analytical wants to hear: Benefits outweigh costs, margins are in line or better than current products.

This strategy will create "in demand" products for dentists' highest profit customers—seniors who need crowns and bridges. That opens the door for us to every dental office in the country. Through two distributors, we surveyed 15 dentists who bought our new product line who previously were not customers. Every one bought because our products were "senior friendly." This strategy capitalizes on our success and can expand sales and margins with a cost that is 50 to 75 percent of our current costs of introducing another new line.

Conservative or hostile needs to hear: Standing still will cost the company.

We have an opportunity of the size and magnitude we aren't likely to see again soon—our competitors will match our product in two to three years. The question is how can we utilize our window to develop a strategic competitive advantage? Developing a "senior" product group with a wide range of advisors gives us a strong opportunity to lock up the market.

Addressing New Opportunities

The description of the situation and the proposed strategy are:

Social networking sites are exploding on the Internet and the company may lose sales because of management and marketing's lack of involvement in this arena. The strategy I'm proposing is to set up social network pages on Facebook and MySpace named after the store, Barry's Electronic Network, and have 10 to 12 young sales associates for each product category for example photography, games, music downloads, and others. We can post notes about new products, show cool ways to use products, give tips, and receive customer comments. The pages would be open to everyone and team members would take turns responding to customer entries.

Higher management wants to hear: Strategy provides significant potential benefits, also increases in profits and margins.

Young people, from 12 to 28, are a significant, highly profitable part of our customer base and this strategy will let us take a leadership role in reaching them through a new medium. The input from the market should help us know what new products to stock and how to sell those products, increasing our sales and profits.

Action-oriented wants to hear: Opportunity can be exploited quickly with little internal turmoil.

We have surveyed the younger members of our retail team and over 80 percent are already active on social networking sites and they fully understand how to interact on the proposed sites. These kinds of Web pages don't require any involvement from the IT department. Our teams of sales associates already know how to create social networking pages in just a few hours and they understand how to promote our page within the social networking sites.

Analytical wants to hear: Upside probabilities trump downside risks.

The downside risk is that customers can criticize the company in an open forum. The upside is our associates will be able to pass that criticism on to the marketing department where adjustments can be made, and they also can respond directly to the criticism suggesting solutions to customers. The program's cost is small and the upside to an important customer group is enormous.

Conservative or hostile needs to hear: Risk of inaction is high.

Someone in our industry will move to create social networking pages. Already companies in the gaming, music, and cell phone industries—industries with close ties to our company—are moving forward with their own pages to promote their products and collect customer data. The question is: Do we want to lead or follow? The strategy can be easily implemented and not being first will hurt us in the market. We need to move ahead.

Internal Strategies

Internal strategies are often not as exciting to present as external, but they will make up many of the strategies you will prepare in your career. The problem in presenting an internal strategy is to get people to say yes on a decision they may not consider to be as important as an external strategy. The best solution is to resolve as many issues as possible regarding implementation before presenting the strategy.

Solving a Problem

The description of the strategy that solves a problem is:

> We currently have between 30 to 100 on-call workers at big events at the convention center. When multiple events are running, scheduling those workers is a problem, as we don't have a good method of tracking people and knowing when they are committed. At the last Industry Convention a new software staffing program was developed that coordinated available people with the events being run. The program also automatically notified people through email and recorded their availability when they responded. I recommend we purchase this

software and improve the use of our on-call staff at our customer training events.

Higher management wants to hear: Others agree this is the right approach; assurance that the solution will solve the problem.

Our staffing and IT departments both feel this new software is a good choice, and the general consensus is that if the software could handle the Industry Convention, it can certainly handle any amount of business that we will see.

Action-oriented wants to hear: Others have implemented similar solutions without any major problems.

The Industry Convention event schedulers used the software to be sure they had enough people at each event as well as handling workers at the various press parties and events that occurred both before and during the convention. The software had a few bugs before the convention but they were all resolved before its start.

Analytical wants to hear: The problem will be solved cost efficiently.

The software package is $8,000. Our event personnel planners feel they will save this money in four months by not having to schedule extra people at events.

Conservative or hostile needs to hear: High probability of success, potentially bad consequences for those who resist.

This software has been proven at both the Industry Convention and at several other convention centers. The software will eliminate the mad panic staffing has before every event. We need to move ahead as the staff feels it cuts turnover by eliminating the hassles that make their jobs difficult. It also will help keep our on-call workers available as they will have better notification of when they are needed.

Improving Performance

The description of the situation and statement of strategy are:

Our company has been expanding rapidly and we have been hiring people to fill in the gaps and get the work out but we have evolved to a sort of helter-skelter approach where we only attack the most pressing issue. I'm proposing we implement a new strategy where we adopt the Lean Manufacturing approach of having a standard work statement for each employee. This will help us ensure that every task is addressed in a timely manner.

Higher management wants to hear: Increased profitability and improved customer satisfaction.

Improving our ability to attack all tasks in a timely fashion will enable us to improve employee productivity, which will keep our staffing levels down and ensure we are on time meeting customer requirements.

Action-oriented wants to hear: Strategy will be successful and accepted by others; will build company momentum.

Most, if not all, the employees recognize that we are letting tasks fall by the wayside as more critical projects receive priority attention. Employees want to see the situation under control and I believe developing standard

work procedures for each job will create a feeling of
momentum.

Analytical wants to hear: Cost benefit analysis; program
won't be disruptive.

I've found a consultant who has extensive experience
implementing standard work standards and he can train
two people to create new standards for all. I expect it will
take two to three months to prepare all the standards and
the cost for the consultant would be $5,000. We are so
disorganized at the moment that we aren't sure of the
exact cost savings from the program but I'm convinced it
will have no more than a six-month payback period.

Conservative or hostile needs to hear: The risks of not
implementing the strategy are greater than the risk of
moving forward.

As a small company we were able to handle the lack of
work standards. But as we've grown we have shifted from
chaos level to the point where we are in danger of
complete grid lock. We will turn out less than 50 percent
of the work we should be able to produce.

Creating a Strategic Advantage

The description of the situation and proposed strategy are:

We have six competitors in the sports stadium
construction market, and the goal of every company is to
have the best on-time under-budget performance, a goal
now missed by the industry on over 60 percent of
ongoing projects. We have already implemented a
software program with modeling capability to help us bid

and build projects. I'm proposing that we take the modeling concept one step further and add the capability of building a project on the computer, step by step. That will allow us to know exactly what work will be done on a specific project and the week on which it needs to be completed. We will be able to better plan work staff and material purchases to keep costs down and projects on schedule.

Higher management wants to hear: Higher profits, more sales, and a better reputation.

This strategy gives us a capability no one else in the industry has, and it is targeted at two points extremely important to customers: timeliness and on-budget completion of projects. The new software, which we will develop, will help keep our costs down, deliver supplies on an as-needed basis, but most importantly, turn us into the preeminent supplier in the market.

Action-oriented wants to hear: Implementation will not cause disruption in operations; implementation will be successful.

We have a relationship with the local university to prepare the software upgrade. They helped us prepare the original modeling software and have already been experimenting with new features. They are confident that they can have the new upgrades in place and debugged in four months.

Analytical wants to hear: Strong benefits to justify costs and risks.

Our project managers have identified three major savings from this type of software upgrade: (1) it would minimize lost time if supplies aren't in place on time; (2) it would minimize losses or damage that occurs because parts and supplies arrive too early; and (3) it would eliminate the extra time in moving materials around supplies that are present but not yet needed. People who have reviewed this option all believe we will have major improvements in cost control and on-time delivery.

Conservative or hostile needs to hear: Risks of not proceeding are high.

Last year we ended up with 40 percent overtime on the last two months of four projects, and we absorbed over $1 million in cost overruns. We can't cut these costs down unless we implement this new modeling strategy.

Addressing New Opportunities

The description of the situation and the proposed strategy are:

We have not been able to pick up large orders from vehicle manufacturers because we have not shown that we can deliver products with consistent quality. I recommend we adopt the new training process from TWI. We can reserve every other Thursday for training for supervisors on production efficiency, and every Friday to teach employees how to effectively operate their equipment with the goal of reducing variation and fluctuations in our product quality.

Higher management wants to hear: Strategy will lead to revenues and profits to overcome the costs.

Our competitors with similar equipment have been able to land the major business by focusing on continuous improvement in their processes. Our company has been loaded with orders over the past two years and we haven't had the time to make the same type of commitment to process improvements. Our inability to focus our resources has let some of the competitors leapfrog us in sales. We need to catch up, which will position the company to land bigger, more profitable orders in upcoming years when the economy picks up.

Action-oriented wants to hear: Successful implementation without internal resistance.

We can contract with a quality control consulting firm to start the implementation process. The supervisors I've spoken with support the program because they expect layoffs if we don't start landing some major orders.

Analytical wants to hear: Likely success with a result that is worth the effort.

We can't afford the expansions we need to keep our market share without landing at least some new business from our major customers. This new training process gives us the opportunity to upgrade our process control and product quality. Our competitors have grown 40 percent by landing this business. Recouping our costs will be in less than 12 months once we land a major customer.

Conservative or hostile needs to hear: The risks of not acting are great.

Three years ago our quality was acceptable to all companies in the market. The two major customers have raised the quality bar and demanded more quality process than we currently have. We have to expect other customers to do the same. If we stand still and don't take this chance to standardize our processes and product we many start losing customers and then it will be too late to reengineer the company.

Chapter 4

Address Listeners' Expected Concerns

I n many cases you'll be presenting to people who have strong views about the situation that your strategy addresses and they might be predisposed to prefer another strategy, or be skeptical about the effectiveness of your strategy. At this point, before going more into the benefits of your presentation, you should address those concerns directly and forcefully. This will give your listeners a chance to challenge you, or challenge themselves on whether or not their concerns are valid.

External Strategies

Solving a Problem

Higher management wants to hear: Is the proposed strategy a complete solution; is it the best solution available; will it detract from other company efforts?

I know the company doesn't want to rush into action, and possibly not solve the problem or create more problems. Our strategy is based on conversations with several key market contacts about their concerns and how they suggest we respond. Another benefit of this strategy is that it can be implemented by a small group and therefore won't upset the effectiveness of any of the company's other market initiatives.

Action-oriented wants to hear: Implementation will not bog down and distract other company efforts.

I'm confident we can implement the solution with a team of four people. Before we move ahead we will be sure to have the plan agreed to by the most involved managers so that the program goes forward smoothly.

Analytical wants to hear: The strategy hasn't been thoroughly analyzed; not enough cost analysis has been done.

In moving quickly to resolve the problem the danger is in moving too fast and not anticipating the true cost of the program. I have a preliminary plan and costs worked out but before implementing the plan we will finalize more details and work with accounting to establish the final costs. If they are not in line with our current projections we will come back and present the strategy to you again.

Conservative or hostile needs to hear: Moving forward will be worse than our current situation.

I know that action for action's sake is not acceptable. We must be improving the situation dramatically to make the strategy worthwhile. My follow-up conversations with customers have indicated that this problem is perceived by customers to be significant. I'm convinced we must act, and that our strategy addresses the key issues customers have told me.

Improving Performance

Higher management wants to hear: Will this strategy really make a difference, both to the market and our bottom line?

I realize we only can introduce a few new programs to the market every year, and that we need to be sure they have a big impact, and don't delay other important programs. At the moment we don't have any other major programs to introduce, and I believe this strategy has the potential for a 15 percent revenue increase.

Action-oriented wants to hear: The strategy needs to be important; can the strategy be quickly implemented?

We need market momentum and I realize you want to see a program have the visibility to produce that impact. This strategy will be the first in the market that offers a total solution for this application. Customers have been requesting it for two years and we can have it in the market in less than six months.

Analytical wants to hear: Has the decision been studied carefully; have margins and market acceptance been considered?

We chose this strategy because it has high value to the market. Our surveys indicate we will be able to generate a

58 percent margin, which is 15 percent higher than our current product line.

Conservative or hostile needs to hear: New programs could create problems; program will detract from other proposed programs.

I know others may have proposed programs, but I believe this strategy sets the bar high. The program is supported by the marketing and sales departments; initial market feedback is we will become a leader in the target market, and our margins on sales will be 5 percent higher.

Creating a Strategic Advantage

Higher management wants to hear: Will the advantage translate to a decidedly stronger market position or be a wasted effort?

I realize the company is not interested in implementing a strategic advantage strategy that doesn't have a major impact. This strategy has a major impact because first, it positions us as the leader in the fastest growing application in the market; second, it is adopting technology on an exclusive basis; and third, adding this technology will allow us to entice the leading distributors in the market to carry our line exclusively.

Action-oriented wants to hear: The company will not get bogged down trying to implement a major new program.

I realize that despite the fact this strategy is a major program, we run the risk of a sluggish introduction which could deaden its impact. I have prepared a plan for the introduction of this program that includes a three-person task force that will work out all the implementation details.

Analytical wants to hear: Strategy will not consume resources without producing significant positive results.

A key question is, will we get a return on an investment that consumes a major portion of our resources? The strategic advantage we are developing relates to an application that is small today but will be a major percentage of sales in two years. The investment we are making will increase our market position for at least two years before any competitor can respond.

Conservative or hostile needs to hear: Program will work out and the company will be better off than before.

The benefits of the program are strong, but there are also risks if the program doesn't work out. The first step of our implementation plan is to present the strategy to our sales force's advisory council, which consists of 10 key customers, to get their input about the market's response to our program, and to ensure we have acceptance before proceeding.

Addressing New Opportunities

Higher management wants to hear: Do we have the ability to capitalize on this opportunity?

The concern is that the company can't raise enough money or find the right people to exploit this opportunity. I've put together a cash flow analysis of the project and it only uses half the money that finance has stated it can raise for new projects. Regarding key people to capitalize on the opportunity: for internal people, I have identified one other key person who can lead the team, and I've found two outside people we can use to rapidly exploit this opportunity.

Action-oriented wants to hear: We will not expend effort and energy without being able to exploit the opportunity.

I realize pursuing new opportunities often takes more time, money, and people than originally projected. I don't think that is the case here. The finance department has indicated this project will only take 25 percent of the money we have earmarked for exploring revenue enhancement and we have a group of employees perfectly suited to quickly move forward.

Analytical wants to hear: Is the opportunity as big and as profitable as it's being projected?

Before presenting the strategy, I met with the marketing and finance departments to prepare an initial financial analysis based on 50 percent of the marketing department's projections. We went over the projections three times, trying to build a model taking into account any of the key risks, and we still find pursuing the opportunity passes every profitability test.

Conservative or hostile needs to hear: Efforts will not fail; company will be better off than it would be by not taking action.

There is always a risk the program will fail. But for this strategy we have taken numerous precautions: We have received positive customer and market feedback indicating this strategy is a good opportunity; we have cut our risks by partnering with a company with a complementary product, and we have a team of our top people ready to plan and then implement our strategy.

Internal Strategies

People have many concerns with an external strategy because the risks of failure are high, the costs may be higher, only a few major strategies can be pursued in any given year and, more importantly, a poorly thought our external strategy may be remembered by the market for years. You don't have to work nearly as hard to present an internal strategy unless it is expensive.

Solving a Problem

Higher management wants to hear: The problem will be solved; the costs will be in line with what has been projected.

I've been working with a three-person task team from the IT and marketing departments and we all agree this solution will correct the problem. Our cost estimate includes a 30 percent overrun of our expected expenses.

Action-oriented wants to hear: Implementation will not be slow and messy.

If we form a small team of people from each department we can prepare for implementation in two months and complete the changeover in two weeks.

Analytical wants to hear: Every consequence has been considered.

I've spoken with my peers in effected departments to make a list of everything that might go wrong. I'll cover those consequences in the implementation plan for the strategy.

Conservative or hostile needs to hear: Is it worthwhile moving ahead?

Our company objective is to reduce order fulfillment costs by 20 percent. This strategy will cut costs 25 to 30 percent and meet that objective. If we don't move ahead, we will have to spend several months to create another strategy that may not be as effective.

Improving Performance

Higher management wants to hear: Does the strategy meet company objectives; does it delay other key programs?

This strategy both helps meet our cost-cutting objectives— it alone will meet 20 percent of those objectives—plus it will free up some key personnel to aggressively address other pertinent, non-cost-cutting issues.

Action-oriented wants to hear: Strategy will not be perceived to be disruptive by other employees and cause turmoil.

This strategy addresses a major concern voiced by numerous employees in the affected area over the past two years. It will provide a major morale boost that should improve productivity.

Analytical wants to hear: Company is not moving too fast; this will be the best process with the highest impact.

Our group has prepared an evaluation grid of all the operational improvements we could pursue this year. We considered costs, both financial and manpower, benefits, and implementation time. The strategy we are proposing is the clear winner when considering all categories.

Conservative or hostile needs to hear: This is the strategy they favor; prefers not to stay with the status quo but instead to move forward.

We have an objective this year for cutting our time to respond to customer inquiries by 50 percent. We can't meet that goal without acting soon. I feel this proposal will meet that goal. No one else has put any strategies on the table so I feel we need to move ahead.

Creating a Strategic Advantage

Internal strategies that create a strategic advantage typically require extensive resources and are major decisions. You need to work hard to sell an internal strategy that offers a strategic advantage because people will know it can only be created with a major effort by the company. You can do that by showing the effort isn't as major as people expect or will produce benefits that will make the effort worthwhile.

Higher management wants to hear: Will the strategy really produce higher profits?

The $2,000 car, the Nano, by Tata Motors in India, was made possible by designing the product from the ground up. We could take the same approach on line x, where the industry's costs are too high for the product's benefits.

A new design, with a drop in costs, would put us far ahead of our competition in this important market.

Action-oriented wants to hear: The project will not take too long; it will provide enough benefits.

Our product has not been redesigned for six years. Over the years engineers have put forward several projects to redesign certain aspects of the product. We could incorporate those proposals in the project to cut its delivery time and costs.

Analytical wants to hear: There is not too much uncertainty in the project; strategy is certain to produce the project's benefits.

Clearly the project is tackling a major goal. If we achieve this goal we will have a several-year advantage over competition as they do not have the same engineering resources that we do. The engineering department has two new engineers who have done a similar project at their previous companies and they are confident they can succeed here. The expected cost reduction is 50 to 65 percent.

Conservative or hostile needs to hear: The project is not too big or too risky.

This strategy implementation is a big project and if it is not completed we will have squandered a considerable amount of our resources. But this idea is not totally new—different groups have been looking at different versions of this concept for the last three years and the project team has a firm idea on how to move ahead. Everyone involved is confident the project can be completed.

Addressing New Opportunities

New internal strategies are typically implementing new products, technologies, or processes.

Higher management wants to hear: Is the opportunity as important when it is evaluated against other opportunities? Do the benefits justify the costs?

We have objectives for updating our internal operations and several other groups have or will have proposals for meeting those objectives. I believe this is the strategy to pursue for three reasons: Its savings will cover our introduction costs in six months; we have two people on staff who have training from seminars and conferences on implementing this tactic; and the project is ready to go right now.

Action-oriented wants to hear: Can it be implemented without internal resistance?

Other groups in the company have other proposals they are promoting, but our strategy is the only one that can be implemented in less than three months. While others will be disappointed, they all understand that this is the only project that can meet the company's timeline goals.

Analytical wants to hear: Is the strategy well thought out with regard to the cost-benefit analysis?

This strategy has been studied thoroughly. We have explored this concept at conferences, had a consultant conduct a study to see if the strategy would work in our company, and have prepared a financial analysis that demonstrates a 40 percent yearly profit on our investment. All data indicate that this will be a very successful, profitable project.

Conservative or hostile needs to hear: If this project fails, it might reduce the chances of other projects or strategies being launched.

People who have reviewed the strategy to date all feel it will succeed. The strategy is based on projects that have been successfully implemented and we do have people with the skill and experience set to introduce it. More importantly, because the project is well defined, it should be completed quickly and still allow the company to pursue additional opportunities this year.

Chapter 5

Show the Strategy as a Response

I once heard a speaker state that fear of loss is ten times more powerful as a motivator than opportunity for gain. While that is not true for everyone, I've learned it is true for many. Companies are much more willing to respond to internal or external events than they are to break new ground. I've seen strategies to solve a problem adopted, which are clearly a response, over innovative strategies that broke new ground and offered two to three times the benefit. The minivan, one of the great product introduction stories of the last 30 years, was a desperate response to the fact that Chrysler was about to go broke. Apple, which is generally known for innovation, introduced the iPod as a response to other MP3 players. I've found people are more comfortable when you can show that your strategy is a response to a situation, and your best approach to prove the situation requires a response is to make the situation as urgent as possible.

External Strategies

Positioning your strategy as a response is easily done for most external strategies as your markets and competitors constantly change, thereby demanding new actions.

Solving a Problem

Higher management wants to hear: Solution addresses a major problem.

This is an important step for our company as the strategy is a response to a problem our vendors, distributors, and customers have complained about.

Action-oriented wants to hear: Solution is a quick response to silence market criticism.

This strategy provides a quick response that will silence our market critics, and the response is so fast that the market may quickly forget about this problem.

Analytical wants to hear: The company needs a quick response or more damage may occur.

The strategy provides the quick response to market complaints; we need to avoid bigger problems that will come with a much higher price tag.

Conservative or hostile needs to hear: It is critical that the company responds to the situation.

You have probably seen the reports from the field about the challenges we face due to this problem. Unfortunately we are facing what could soon be a critical situation. We need to respond now.

Improving Performance

Higher management wants to hear: The market is looking for a performance response from the company; the issue is important.

Our installation quality and service has been in the top 50 percent of the market for the last five years. But now competitors are improving their installation departments, as well as the simplicity of their products. We need to respond. The proposed strategy will noticeably raise our perceived quality of installation.

Action-oriented wants to hear: The strategy is a quick response to the situation.

This strategy is a direct response to customers' concern that we need to upgrade our service network. We believe our plan will meet customers' expectations within four months.

Analytical wants to hear: We understand the situation; we are responding.

This strategy is responding to the high costs we are facing with current vendors. Both engineering and marketing have been involved in reviewing our three best options and we all believe this strategy is the best choice considering margins, market acceptance, and vendor qualification.

Conservative or hostile needs to hear: Responding to the market needs is crucial.

This strategy to improve our performance is a direct response to the new changes in the distribution strategy from our competitors. We need to match that improvement or we are going to lose market penetration.

Creating a Strategic Advantage

Solving problems and process improvements are typically smaller, more operational strategies. Strategic advantages deal with bigger issues, and are responding generally in bigger ways, but they still should be explained as a response to market changes.

Higher management wants to hear: The situation the strategy is responding to is real and important.

This strategy will put the company in a leadership role in the market as it changes because of the new government mandates for renewable energy. Those mandates are already in place to take effect in two years. Our proposed strategy will allow us to lock up major distributors if we move now.

Action-oriented wants to hear: The situation demands an immediate response.

Our proposed strategy will allow us to lock up major distributors if we move now. Our competitors may introduce their strategies in the next three months, if we wait we may be too late.

Analytical wants to hear: Competitive responses to the situation have been considered.

The situation the strategy addresses has given us a window of opportunity in our response. Our competitors are either committed to a new program with financial institutions or involved in combining operations after a merger to respond quickly to this market change.

Conservative or hostile needs to hear: Company must respond.

Our competition has gained the upper hand with more complete offerings then we have. We need to respond. We can either play catch-up on our product line, or we can use the strategy to seize a strategic advantage in this crucial area to solidify the company's future.

Addressing New Opportunities

Higher management wants to hear: Response is a significant opportunity with a key market segment.

The strategy addresses an opportunity that is most important to the market innovators. The rest of the market has always followed the innovators after 12 to 18 months. If we improve our position now with the innovators, we may dominate the market for two to three years.

Action-oriented wants to hear: The response will be immediate and noticeable.

This strategy will be responding to the opportunity within two months, and we will be able to announce it three months before the industry's biggest trade show.

Analytical wants to hear: The opportunity is proven.

The strategy is a response to (name the opportunity). I've spent the last three months at conferences and trade shows evaluating this opportunity against others. I'm convinced the data shows that this opportunity is the biggest one coming into the market over the next two years.

Conservative or hostile needs to hear: Not moving on the opportunity will hurt the company's image.

After years of stability, the market is changing rapidly and there are many opportunities to pursue. This one is large, and well suited to our market position. If we don't respond, we will be considered too conservative and traditional to respond to the market's needs.

Internal Strategies

Solving a problem is obviously a response to a situation. But you will also be more effective if you can explain other strategies as a response.

Solving a Problem

Higher management wants to hear: Strategy addresses all the issues raised.

In creating the strategy, we wanted our response to the problem to be more than a stop-gap solution and get to the root of what causes the problem. Our strategy is a little more involved than just removing the symptom, but it minimizes the chance of a similar problem occurring in the future.

Action-oriented wants to hear: Strategy solves the problem with minimal disruption.

We can put the strategy in place over a three-day period, responding quickly to the problem that has arisen, while minimizing any disruption to our normal work flow.

Analytical wants to hear: The response won't create other problems.

Our strategy is responding to the problem we've seen in the operations department. Before recommending implementation, we evaluated the impact of work flow two steps before and after the step where we implemented our strategy. We are convinced that the change we are proposing will be seamless with the department's work flow.

Conservative or hostile needs to hear: The organizational consensus is that the problem must be solved quickly.

I'm trying to move ahead with our strategy as quickly as possible as a response to this problem. People in the organization have made solving the problem a top priority.

Improving Performance

Higher management wants to hear: Performance improvement addresses a key area.

The strategy we are suggesting, putting needed information on the Web site, will cut our costs of providing managers with financial data by 50 percent, while improving managers' access to the information they need. This strategy is responding to a key need of coordinating managers' decisions to meet the company's financial goals.

Action-oriented wants to hear: The need for the strategy is clear; responses will be supported.

This strategy is directed at an area that has already been designated as needing continuous improvement. This response is far better than others proposed and will improve the process flow 15 percent without increasing the work force.

Analytical wants to hear: Response was well thought out.

Before suggesting this strategy I observed the current process for eight hours over a two-week period and identified the steps where we could make substantial improvements. Our response addresses an area targeted by the company plan for improvement.

Conservative or hostile needs to hear: Improvement is far better than any other alternatives.

I've attended several meetings where the need for improvements in this area have been detailed and where proposed strategies have been requested. No one has come forward, and the strategy I'm proposing beats the targeted improvement goal by 50 percent.

Creating a Strategic Advantage

Higher management wants to hear: The situation requiring a response is major.

This strategy is a response to people's interest in a "green" home. There is a need for an easy-to-use informational site. Repositioning and redesigning our Web site as the first comprehensive, green home site will allow us and our franchisees to capture a large percentage of people changing over to green right at the point of conversion.

Action-oriented wants to hear: Response to the situation in a way that generates a strategic advantage will energize the organization.

One of the key advantages of this strategy is that our staff will immediately see that this response to green packaging issues has the potential to radically change the way our company is perceived.

Analytical wants to hear: The response will clearly lead to a strategic advantage.

We evaluated carefully whether or not our internal response would lead to a strategic advantage. We asked: Are we more capable of implementing this strategy; are competitors tied up with other projects; and is the market likely to value our advantage for a long time? The answer to all these questions was yes.

Conservative or hostile needs to hear: The response won't jeopardize the company's future.

One positive aspect of our strategy is that it is relatively easy to implement and if it doesn't produce the desired result it still creates process improvements in the three operational areas that have been identified as bottlenecks in our production process.

Addressing New Opportunities

Higher management wants to hear: Pursuing the new opportunity helps respond to an identified company weakness.

We are recommending this approach because the targeted department hasn't improved its procedures significantly in five years. Adopting the new strategy will force the department to start by paring down its procedures to the bare minimum. At other companies this process has streamlined procedures by as much as 50 percent.

Action-oriented wants to hear: Others feel strongly that a response is needed.

Others have noticed that our competitors operate with 30 to 40 percent of the employees in their similar departments. We can get down to those staffing levels if we take advantage of the new service being offered by the state.

Analytical wants to hear: The response has been proven to be an improvement.

We are responding to a situation in the (name the department) where our turnaround time is too slow. To be sure the response is an improvement, we checked with five companies that have implemented this strategy. All five stated that their turnaround times were significantly improved.

Conservative or hostile needs to hear: There is almost an overwhelming need to respond to the situation.

This strategy is responding to the steady slow down in work from the (name the department). Adding more personnel hasn't helped and only a total overhaul will correct the situation. We've searched for a way to do that and implementing this new development will turn the situation around.

Chapter 6

Demonstrate a Good Fit

You will typically be more successful presenting strategies if you can show that your proposals are a good fit for your current operations and personnel. For example, a good fit for a company that designs and prints direct mail flyers for financial institutions would be a strategy that changes how it bills customers from charging for the work completed to charging based on the responses generated by a direct mail campaign. The company wouldn't need to change how it prints or designs pieces and it is a strategy the company could easily implement. The company would probably produce more income if it created effective campaigns.

An example of a strategy with a questionable fit would be for a company that manufactures cryogenic tanks for storing oxygen at hospitals to decide to produce hydrogen cryogenic storage tanks for fuel cell vehicles. The company might understand how to make cryogenic tanks, but it wouldn't understand the requirements for installing them on vehicles, would not have the proper installation and service people on staff, and would not have the right marketing and salespeople in place.

If your strategy is not a good fit, then you need to do your best to show that the organization can easily adopt the changes required to pursue your recommended strategy.

External Strategies

For external strategies, the good fit can relate to your target market, perceived strengths, sales and marketing departments, distribution network, service and installation capabilities, or key customer relationships.

Solving a Problem

Higher management wants to hear: Staffing and procedures can handle the strategy.

This strategy fits into the existing procedural framework for technical support. We will need to add just one person to the technical service department.

Action-oriented wants to hear: Strategy can be implemented easily.

We can implement our strategy with our current staff by reassigning people from distributors support to key customer support.

Analytical wants to hear: The impact on the organization has been considered.

I've looked at the impact of the strategy on all three affected departments. In all cases their current procedures with minor modifications can handle all the work required.

Conservative or hostile needs to hear: The strategy will cause, at the most, minor disruptions.

The strategy fits right into our current operations and we can implement the program without disrupting any of our operations.

Improving Performance

Higher management wants to hear: Strategy fits into long-term goals; minor disruption to operations.

This strategy is aligned with the company's goal of being premium supplier for our target market. The plant has space to incorporate this new production and technical service will be ready with a week's worth of training.

Action-oriented wants to hear: Everyone is on board for a quick implementation.

The four effected departments are all excited about improving our performance and they all are developing a plan to complete their part of the project.

Analytical wants to hear: The strategy has been evaluated to be sure it has the best possible fit to the company.

We were able to change our original version of the strategy so it reinforced our branding strategy and our customers' positive perception of our services. It is a good fit for the company's capabilities.

Conservative or hostile needs to hear: No one is complaining; it will be a seamless introduction.

Some changes in our sales department are required, but that shouldn't present a problem as the strategy helps sales meet its one- and three-year goals.

Creating a Strategic Advantage

Strategic advantage strategies typically require a major effort that is almost always somewhat to very disruptive. What you want to concentrate on is that the strategy fits the company's goals or is an important step to keeping your customer base.

Higher management wants to hear: The company will grow within the framework of its stated goals and objectives.

A real benefit of this program is that it fits exactly with the company's stated vision of where the market will develop and leaves us with the opportunity to become one of the market's top three suppliers.

Action-oriented wants to hear: The company will be able to quickly reorganize; the market will recognize the benefits.

A key to this strategy is that the customers will immediately see its importance to them, and we won't need an expensive marketing program as it is a natural extension of all our current efforts.

Analytical wants to hear: A balance has been struck between the market advantage the company could gain versus the effort required from reorganizing to generate that benefit.

In preparing this strategy I looked at the benefit, the advantage we could gain, versus the risk, and how much effort the organization would require for implementation. The balance I've chosen provides for substantial gain with only moderate changes in our current operations.

Conservative or hostile needs to hear: Every effort has been made to ensure the strategy is as close a fit as possible.

I spent considerable time contemplating how to gain the advantage while ensuring the strategy causes a minimum number of organizational changes. After changing the action plan a few times I believe I've structured the strategy so it fits our marketing message and reinforces our relationship with our key customers.

Addressing New Opportunities

Higher management wants to hear: Opportunity is in line with the company's overall strategy; fits in with company capabilities.

This opportunity adds to our branding strategy of the industry's leading innovator. It is targeted at our second-largest market and can be implemented with just two new hires.

Action-oriented wants to hear: The strategy is easy to implement; has a synergistic effect on other services or products.

We can implement this strategy with our current staff, but what makes this opportunity particularly appealing is it will allow us to expand our distribution network, an addition that will increase sales of our entire product line.

Analytical wants to hear: A preliminary action plan has been prepared which defines the organizational requirements.

We have completed a study of the changes and workerpower needed to pursue this opportunity. We only require a few changes as our organizational structure is an almost ideal fit for this opportunity.

Conservative or hostile needs to hear: Similar opportunities in the past were overlooked because the guidelines for a good organizational fit were too tight.

In the past the company has passed on several opportunities. (It is a good idea to list one or two of those opportunities.) The reason given was they were not a good fit for our company. Other companies took advantage of the opportunities and have done well. We can't afford to pass on opportunities because we are looking for a 100 percent perfect fit.

Internal Strategies

Unless companies perceive they have severe problems in their internal organization, they prefer incremental change. You can help sell the internal strategy by demonstrating the change will only affect a narrow range of employees or operations—for example, the change will only impact the order entry department's process for taking orders from key customers—or by giving examples of how the company has adopted similar strategies in other areas.

Solving a Problem

Higher management wants to hear: The approach is similar to how we have successfully approached problems in the past.

The strategy we are following is the same one that was used in our San Francisco and Salt Lake offices for very similar problems.

Action-oriented wants to hear: Managers involved in the change have successfully tackled other similar projects.

There are two managers involved in this corrective action and both have used similar methodology to solve other problems in the past.

Analytical wants to hear: Options have been reviewed that consider both the solution and its fit with the organization.

We've considered several approaches to the problem and feel the one we proposed is an effective solution that can be implemented without any organizational changes.

Conservative or hostile needs to hear: The solution will require either minor or no organizational changes; others support the strategy.

I've discussed this strategy with others (name them) and they also feel this solution will be effective and anticipate that the strategy can be implemented with a simple engineering change in the quality control inspection process.

Improving Performance

Higher management wants to hear: The strategy fits into the overall organization continual improvement goals.

Improving the work order format for incoming service jobs was one of the company's top three priorities for the year in our Lean Manufacturing continuous improvement program.

Action-oriented wants to hear: The strategy can be implemented with only minor disruptions.

This strategy closely fits our current operations, we only need to add three paperwork changes and have a two-day training program for four people.

Analytical wants to hear: An effort has been made to ensure that the transition will be smooth.

I researched our other offices and found five other instances of offices implementing similar improvement strategies with only minor implementation problems.

Conservative or hostile needs to hear: The improvement is in a key area; the solution requires only minor changes.

Our department needs to show leadership incorporating the newest changes to proposed industry quality standards. This strategy starts by adding technology that our testing facility is familiar with and which over 50 percent of the staff has already used in other jobs.

Creating a Strategic Advantage

A strategic advantage usually requires change, sometimes major change, in how an internal organization is run. When promoting an internal change that may be major, your focus should be on how the strategy takes advantage of the organization's core strengths.

Higher management wants to hear: The changes involved will be made by the company's top performers.

Our company has always had an innovative and strong design engineering group. Putting that group in charge of this strategy is key, as our production equipment will need a level of modification that is beyond our production engineering department capabilities.

Action-oriented wants to hear: The path to introduce this new strategy is clear and the people to do the job have been identified.

Our Web team has always kept the company's site two or three steps ahead of our competition. The new strategy delivers a whole new benefit package to consumers. We are able to implement the strategy, well before competitors can respond, because of the well-known strength of our Web development team.

Analytical wants to hear: We have carefully thought out who should be implementing the strategy.

This strategy was chosen because it is a strategy that will be delivered by the marketing group, our strongest department. We had other strategy choices, some that were equally as strong, but felt our best chance for profitable growth was to put a program on the back of our most effective department.

Conservative or hostile needs to hear: The implementation group is strong enough to overcome obstacles and deliver.

Obviously gaining the type of strategic advantage we need to position ourselves for the future requires a major program with some risks. But the program will be implemented by our strongest department, one that has faced obstacles and overcome them time after time. We will succeed by relying on their very high level of expertise.

Addressing New Opportunities

Higher management wants to hear: We are pursuing an opportunity that improves our operation in (name the department) where improvement is needed; the right staff is in place to help.

This new technology will improve a department that has repeatedly rated below similar departments at other locations. We can borrow a department head from the other location to implement this technology which will provide a major performance increase.

Action-oriented wants to hear: We have the people and plan in place to move ahead.

The trade show and event department has already done four shows as big, or bigger, than this one, and they already have an interactive display that can be converted for the new market application being promoted by the conference. The trade show department can add one or two staff members and be prepared to expand our trade show presence.

Analytical wants to hear: The good fit really exists.

Our department will be implementing the strategy. Two people in the group were the leaders of the last major opportunity to improve our process quality control checks. Two people in the department have already developed a preliminary plan so that this new effort will match their previous success.

Conservative or hostile needs to hear: The company has successfully pursued opportunities of a similar nature in the past.

Our two international offices already implemented similar strategies without any problems, and the new server system has had 40 percent less downtime at those locations.

Part Two

Delivering the Power

This section talks about how to cast your strategy as one that will make a true difference to the corporation, preparing the company for the future, which includes introducing strategies for growing the company, cutting costs, and establishing a stronger presence with key customer groups. Companies typically do not succeed if they adopt strategies that don't contribute to the future. This sounds obvious, but I've heard many strategies that are stop-gap measures, but those types of strategies tend to tie up the company so it doesn't move forward. You'll have much more success in your presentations if you take the time to ensure your strategy strengthens the organization and prepares it for the future.

This section takes a much different tack than Part One, where you make people feel comfortable with the strategy you present. Now you are taking the tact, either implicitly or explicitly, that the company isn't doing well enough, that the company needs to change, and that if it doesn't change in time, it will die. You will be delivering the power, showing how your strategy will help the company succeed in the future.

In some cases you might be working in a company that is totally committed to growth and positioning itself for the future. Then you should review the steps in Part One and focus on the points this section covers. But be careful: There are people who prefer the status quo in every organization, no matter how growth-oriented the company is. Don't overlook Part One or you may find a resistant audience.

Since in this section we are, for the most part, trying to move the company forward, with the exception of higher management, I only use the phrase "wants to hear" with top management and use "needs to hear" with everyone else.

Chapter 7

Explain the Future Fit

Chapter 6 dealt with how your strategy fits the organization today. This chapter transitions into how the strategy also works to develop the company for the future. It is a transitional part of the presentation where you move from keeping your listeners comfortable to having them realize the strategy helps prepare the company for the future. The point here is to make this transition smoothly and start to get people prepared for the upcoming part of the presentation when you will really attack the issue of how the strategy impacts the company's future.

You have to learn to deliver your strategy presentations with power because companies are only capable of introducing a limited number of strategies a year. The strategies that win are ones that help not only today but also into the future, meeting company long-term revenue and profit goals.

Some readers, and some of the people who will listen to your presentation, might agree with the concept for positioning for the future for external strategies, but not for internal strategies. But that is not sufficient; you must improve operations continually and cut costs if you are going to succeed in the future. You need to show a fit for the future on every presentation.

Your company may not have a written growth objective, and it may not be well publicized or even thought out. Then it is your job to quiz your boss, and even top management if you get a chance, to find out what those goals are. You won't be effective presenting your strategies if you don't have a clear idea of how management believes it needs to change and grow for the future.

External Strategies

Solving a Problem

You should start all of the strategies for solving a problem with the phrase "this strategy doesn't just solve an immediate problem; it also takes a step toward our future goals."

- **Higher management** wants to hear: The strategy is aligned with longer-term goals.

  A stated objective by management has been to move into this new market segment. Using this strategy not only solves the current issue but also cuts the production unit's operating costs and will help us set the stage for the introduction of our new line this fall.

- **Action-oriented** needs to hear: The company is moving forward.

  We can't afford to solve this problem in a way that just allows us to make up lost ground. This strategy solves the problem with our major customers and helps us jump back up to where we would have been if this problem hadn't surfaced, and puts us back on track to meet next year's ambitious goals.

Analytical needs to hear: We have done sufficient analysis that the problem will be solved.

This strategy clearly helps position us for how we see the market evolving. We have also checked with our customers and distributors, who all feel this strategy resolves the problem. This strategy kills two birds with one stone, solving the problem and preparing the company for the new market reality.

Conservative or hostile needs to hear: We need to move forward, correcting as we go, or we will fall behind.

This problem is derailing us from our objective of being the first to enter this market. We can't afford to wait until we have every answer; we may need to correct on the fly. The key is that the strategy addresses the problem while keeping us focused on our mid-range growth plans.

Improving Performance

Higher management wants to hear: The improved performance will help the company be prepared for the future.

Currently we are facing two new major companies entering the market over the next three years. Our goal has been to lock up co-marketing agreements with manufacturers of complementary products to make future competitors' market entry more difficult. Realigning our technical service group will allow better service of our major customers, but it will also allow us to customize interface technologies with our co-marketing partners.

Action-oriented needs to hear: This strategy is ideal because it will minimize the need for other improvements in the future.

This strategy of a system design Web site for distributors to use with their customers also is a first step in the company's goal of providing a consumer design site that allows designers to specify our product line. Making this improvement now will allow us to cut the design time of the consumer site in half.

Analytical needs to hear: The specific company goal that the strategy is meeting; no other strategy is a better fit.

Improving the performance of (state the specific improvement) is important to the company goal of penetrating the emerging market (state specific market). We need this improvement to meet our goals this year, but it does double duty preparing us to attack the new market. Other solutions meet our current need but don't have an impact for our future plans.

Conservative or hostile needs to hear: Time is running out to execute plans that prepare the company for the future.

The company has set aggressive goals for the future. Right now, the strategies proposed to meet those goals have been slowed by internal resistance. This strategy makes an improvement we need now and reaches out for our future plans. We need to start moving now or we will have to tell management we won't meet their goals.

Creating a Strategic Advantage

Higher management wants to hear: This advantage meets their long-term goals; it is a strategy stronger than strategies from its leading competition.

The strategy will solidify our position in what we feel will be the second-fastest emerging market. Our three top competitors are all fighting for a key advantage in the fastest emerging market. The second market will grow 40 to 60 percent as fast as the first market, and this strategy will leave us in a strong protected position for this important market segment.

Action-oriented needs to hear: The company has a clear path to its final objective.

We have looked at the strategy's impact on our key objectives over the next three years and with this strategy we will exceed our objectives each year. Five departments are involved in the strategy's implementation, but a task force of one manager from each department will be enough to keep the project on schedule.

Analytical needs to hear: This strategy will fit into other company growth objectives.

The company has three major objectives for growth: (state what they are). This advantage clearly attacks the second objective. But it is also complementary to the other two goals, and it won't conflict with the proposed strategies for those other two goals.

Conservative or hostile needs to hear: The program fits the company's goals well; resistance would be a mistake.

I've looked at this strategy from every direction and it clearly fits exactly with the company's long-term plan. I don't think people will oppose the plan unless they have created a better alternative strategy.

Addressing New Opportunities

Higher management wants to hear: This is a major opportunity; it fits into our company strategy.

Our department keeps a list of opportunities we project will develop in the next two years. We feel this opportunity will be one of the top three because it provides a valued benefit to a new set of customers. It also clearly fits into our strategy of developing two new markets.

Action-oriented needs to hear: This strategy is lined up with company goals; it makes a significant impact on those goals.

This strategy takes a major step toward meeting the company's major objectives. If implemented properly over the next three years we will meet or exceed a major objective that needs to be accomplished to grow the company in the future.

Analytical needs to hear: The green lights for the strategy are far more important than the red lights.

Obviously any strategy that is expected to impact the company for the next three years will have risks. But the green lights, especially its complete fit with the company goals and its alignment with our target customers' requirements, indicates we should move ahead.

Conservative or hostile needs to hear: No other opportunities are in sight that meet the company's objectives as well.

Our company has stiff competition from well-run companies that have strategic growth plans. We must stay at least even and preferably move ahead of them. This opportunity has an enormous upside for us and, frankly, there are no other opportunities we can pursue that will have a similar impact.

Internal Strategies

External strategies have more glamour but don't downplay the importance of internal strategies. True growth and constant realignment of a company with customer goals usually can't be completed without internal strategies that impact the company just as powerfully as external strategies.

Solving a Problem

Higher management wants to hear: The strategy has both short- and long-term ramifications; it fits the company's long-term objectives.

This strategy offers more than a short-term solution for our backorder situation; it provides a new job tracking system. The job tracking system will cut our production time from one week to five days. Shorter turnaround time is a major company long-term goal.

Action-oriented needs to hear: The strategy does meet long-term goals; the company is ready to move on the solution.

This strategy solves our problem but also meets our strategic goal (state the specific goal). We have done most of the groundwork to investigate implementation, and we are convinced we can move forward in two weeks and have the entire solution in place in six months.

Analytical needs to hear: The strategy truly impacts the long-term objective, justifying the effort to move beyond an immediate solution.

The strategy certainly also impacts our long-term objectives. While we don't feel the strategy is a total solution to all company goals, we can meet those objectives if we treat this step as phase one of the solution. We can schedule the implementation of the second phase (state what that will be) in January.

Conservative or hostile needs to hear: A problem is not an excuse for not hitting long-term objectives.

We have made promises about meeting objectives. No one is going to accept a failure to meet our goals because of a problem that has developed. We need to solve this problem while staying on track and this strategy allows us to do both.

Improving Performance

Higher management wants to hear: The improvement has aggressive goals that match the company's stated objectives.

We have wanted to improve the performance of this area for two years. We have searched for a strategy that offers a

75 to 100 percent improvement. We felt we had to have an increase of that magnitude or the company wouldn't be able to meet its goal of cutting costs 40 percent.

Action-oriented needs to hear: The strategy calls for making changes and there are no other choices for meeting the company goals.

I am recommending we take the strategy one step further so that it can meet the company's three-year objectives. These measures are going to require changes in four departments that will take six months to implement. We can't meet the company's longer-term objectives without these changes.

Analytical needs to hear: The strategy does address strategic goals; and there is evidence it will meet those goals.

We can expand this strategy by (state the expansion) so that it will address a key company strategic goal (state the specific goal). We have looked at expected results over three years in a study we completed and we believe the strategy will provide 25 percent of the goal for reducing factory overhead.

Conservative or hostile needs to hear: What is the reason that a perfect fit with the current organization isn't the right solution?

The strategy can be implemented without disrupting the organization, but if we do that we are going to be subject to immediate criticism that we don't have a longer-term view. We need the strategy to demonstrate we understand the company's long-term goals.

Creating a Strategic Advantage

Your company's internal long-term goals should be met with a strategic advantage strategy. This section should strongly point out the connection between your strategy and the goals.

Higher management wants to hear: This strategy perfectly fits the corporation's long-term goals; it can be executed.

Our long-term goal is an open technology architecture that allows all the makers of auxiliary equipment to interface with our equipment. This strategy of creating interface specialists to coordinate the interfacing of auxiliary equipment will simplify a salesperson's job by 50 percent, but the specialists will also be able to give us the feedback we need to quickly design our desired architecture.

Action-oriented needs to hear: The organization is on target with its goals and objectives.

The company is trying to gain a strategic advantage by establishing strong loyalty with independent field designers. This strategy of creating the database of designs that can respond to tabletop touch screen manipulation is a clear first step in creating the loyalty the company seeks.

Analytical needs to hear: Other options have been reviewed and the timetable is expiring.

This strategy is the result of an ongoing effort to find a strategy that meets the company's strategic goals. We spent three months researching a variety of options and this strategy created the best results and required the least amount of resources. We are confident more analysis won't change our results and we need to start moving by the end of this quarter or we won't hit our goal.

Conservative or hostile needs to hear: The strategy offers a chance to meet the strategic objectives with a minimum amount of disruption.

We need to push this strategy one step further so it meets our long-term objectives. This strategy is a big step toward meeting the goals without totally disrupting our operations. Other options offer a more problematic implementation and could derail our timetables.

Addressing New Opportunities

Higher management wants to hear: The new opportunity makes a significant difference in operations that will impact the long-term goals.

The new reorganization of the IT group is the first nonincremental proposal to come out of the administration area for the last three years. It offers a streamlined process that will cut the IT group's cost by 45 percent. This is 20 percent of cuts in administrative costs that were identified in our growth plans.

Action-oriented needs to hear: Pursuing the new opportunity being proposed can be completed without hindering forward movement on the corporate goals.

This opportunity will be implemented by a department that is not involved in the other strategies to meet our customer service goals—realignment of our regional offices and establishing a licensed repair outlet program.

Analytical needs to hear: The company's goal is aggressive and there is enough analysis to justify moving ahead.

This strategy is being proposed because of the company's target of cutting the time to introduce new products from two years to six months. We are going to need multiple strategies to meet that goal. Our analysis of this strategy has been positive and we need it to move forward so we have time to decide on and implement three to four additional strategies.

Conservative or hostile needs to hear: The positives outweigh the negatives; the company needs to make decisions on moving forward or it won't hit its goals.

This strategy calls for a complete implementation of the MRP software, even though a partial implementation would be easier. We need to do this because we want to keep in mind the goal of doubling the output of each plant. The benefits of the strategy have been proven and we need to make a decision now, because if we delay we won't be able to catch up next year.

Chapter 8

Grow the Company

This is the time in your presentation to take a pause, switch your position if you are talking just to one person, or move around the room if you are talking to a larger audience. You will walk around, or switch positions to emphasize that what you are about to say is extremely important. Growing the company is the key factor that should be driving every strategy. Companies that don't grow die, and this is the part of the presentation you never want someone to forget. This is true of every strategy even if it is for a solution to a small problem on the shop floor. A company needs to focus on growth at all times and in all decisions. By now it is clear what your strategy is and how it fits into the corporate structure. The question on your listeners' minds should be whether or not the project is really worth doing.

The balance of the presentation focuses on delivering your strategy with power. The remainder of your presentation should discuss: growth; value to customers; and finally, costs and money. You will have most of your strategies accepted if you can make the transition from "it's a safe idea to implement," which is the focus of the earlier chapters, to "this is a strategy we can't afford to pass on."

Start your statements on growth with a phrase similar to: "Growth is important to the company and I've taken care to create this strategy so that it will play a role in meeting the company's growth objectives."

External Strategies

Solving a Problem

Higher management wants to hear: The strategy does not just solve the problem but positions the company for future growth.

Field input was that we needed a solution. We took the time to interview customers to find out their total needs and we have restructured our processes to better meet the customers' overall needs. This leaves us in a stronger position with customers and gives us a foundation for future growth.

Action-oriented needs to hear: The company is moving forward quickly.

We want to balance the need to move quickly, so we don't negatively impact our market position, and the need is to find a solution that positions us for growth. This strategy does both: It solves the immediate problem in less than 30 days, and we will respond to two unmet customer needs as we implement the entire solution over the next three months.

Analytical needs to hear: We have thoroughly analyzed that the solution meets current needs while opening the door to further growth.

Two people from our department have visited key players in the market. We explained that we were changing our processes to solve the problem but that we wanted to explore how we could change further to increase our business with them. The input we received is the basis of the strategy I've proposed.

Conservative or hostile needs to hear: We can't afford a more limited solution.

This strategy solves a problem and helps us grow. I realize we could have proposed a more limited solution, but then to hit our growth objections we would have had to change our processes again in the next 12 to 18 months.

Improving Performance

Higher management wants to hear: The improved performance is adequate, or more than adequate, for our growth objectives.

Our current growth objectives call for us to grow 100 percent in the next five years and 30 percent this year. The strategy calls for improvements in our sales strategy that will be capable of 40 to 50 percent growth this year, and another 20 percent jump in revenue next year.

Action-oriented needs to hear: This strategy will meet the relevant growth objectives; the strategy implementation can start immediately.

This improvement meets both our growth goals this year and in the next three years. A plan has been worked out for implementation and we can start moving forward in the next two weeks.

Analytical needs to hear: There is enough evidence to support that the improvement will produce the desired results.

I initially learned of this new Web strategy at a conference two years ago. To check on the growth we need, I called up five other people who attended. Two of them had introduced the strategy in their companies; one company produced over 150 percent of the growth we need and the second produced 175 percent.

Conservative or hostile needs to hear: Standing in the way of progress would be a mistake.

This strategy will deliver 50 percent of the growth we need over the next two years. The success of this strategy in the growth of other companies is well documented and the funding for it is available in our growth fund. It has widespread support within the company and no one has proposed a competing strategy to meet our goals.

Creating a Strategic Advantage

A strategic advantage strategy requires effort and any strategy that you introduce must meet, or preferably exceed, the company's goals.

Higher management wants to hear: This advantage meets their long-term goals; it is a strategy stronger than the strategy of the company's leading competition.

Meeting our growth objectives over the next three years is critical as our competitors are also being aggressive in the market. This strategy gives a key strategic advantage with a customer subset where we have long dominated. Our competitors won't challenge us in this customer group if we have this strategic advantage in place.

Action-oriented needs to hear: The company will be able to implement the strategic advantage quickly.

This strategy supplies the strategic advantage we need to grow. One of the company's growth targets is to increase dealer coverage to 95 percent of the market. We can hit that goal with a new financing strategy for new dealers. We have identified target dealers and can implement this strategy in a six-month period.

Analytical needs to hear: A compelling case can be made that this strategy will meet the company growth objectives.

Because this strategy plays such a key role in our growth goals, we have: studied the outcomes of various market scenarios; attended two conferences on the topic; had a research report commissioned from a leading consultant; and interviewed marketing people at two firms that have launched similar programs. Every step of research we have completed indicates this strategy will be successful.

Conservative or hostile needs to hear: The work completed has been thorough; an alternate plan will be required to derail the strategy.

Over the last few months I've worked with four people in my department and six people from other departments to formulate this strategy and all of us believe it is clear this strategy will meet our goals. I believe the only event that could mitigate this strategy is if someone has a better alternative plan.

Addressing New Opportunities

Higher management wants to hear: This opportunity provides enough of the company's growth objectives to justify the effort to pursue it.

If we pursue this opportunity we will open the door to this entire market segment where we currently only have 5 percent market share. Within two years we can introduce four new products that will result in a revenue increase of 15 percent.

Action-oriented needs to hear: The company is in a position to move on this opportunity.

We are ready now to pursue this opportunity. Our sales force already calls on some of the prospects, the prospects already use our distribution channel, and R&D is ready to release the products for production.

Analytical needs to hear: The opportunity is real and the expected growth has been researched.

This opportunity in the market is the result of a shift in everyone's orientation toward green products. Government programs have been enacted that provide funding over the next three years. Our contacts with key environmental groups all feel this market will grow at a rate of 25 to 50 percent per year.

Conservative or hostile needs to hear: The company can only grow by exploring other opportunities.

Our current sales are in a market segment that is growing slowly as the market evolves. There is no way to generate growth in that segment and we must aggressively pursue new opportunities to generate company momentum.

Internal Strategies

Internal strategies are just like external strategies: they need to help the company grow. Internal strategies can also be expensive as they can call for improvements in the organizational processes, and many times require investments. Those investments must be tied to growth.

Solving a Problem

Higher management wants to hear: The problem has been created by growth; solving the problem will encourage rapid growth.

Our expanded national sales from our regional base has overwhelmed our technical support capabilities. We need to realign with regional support centers throughout the country to meet today's needs, and expand the department capabilities to meet our growth over the next two years.

Action-oriented needs to hear: The strategy can be implemented without any trouble; it is ready to go.

This strategy solves our internal problem but also puts us in a good position to increase sales 50 percent by expanding our service capacity. We have identified our key outsourced vendors and are ready to move forward within 30 days.

Analytical needs to hear: There is evidence to support the claims that the solution will meet company objectives.

The Manufacturing Engineering has laid out our production rates if we implement this solution. Their conclusion is we will increase output 20 percent with the same personnel and space requirements. This nets us 30 percent of our three current cost-cutting goals.

Conservative or hostile needs to hear: Consensus has been reached that this strategy should be implemented.

The engineering and marketing personnel who have reviewed this plan all agree it can meet the requirements of solving our current problems as well as contribute significantly to our growth objectives. The strategy has been used by other companies with success and moving now will enable us to get back on budget within 60 days.

Improving Performance

Higher management wants to hear: The improvement stretches the organization in a way that helps accelerate meeting the company goals.

This strategy forces the organization to drop some of the company's legacy policies that have inhibited many changes to the company's culture. The improvement surpasses our goals and institutes a new matrix that will jump start both our productivity and cost-cutting objectives.

Action-oriented needs to hear: The improvement has aggressive goals that match the company's stated objectives.

We've evaluated the strategy in relation to our three-year objectives and three-year action plan and it helps the company meet two of its three objectives and addresses completely three key steps in our three-year action plan.

Analytical needs to hear: The improved performance is clearly the best choice for the company's objectives.

Before recommending this strategy we had several brainstorming sessions with people in relevant departments searching for a list of alternatives. No other strategy offered the same potential to meet our growth objectives nor did any other strategy have the same synergy with our company's core strengths.

Conservative or hostile needs to hear: There is no backup plan to meet the company objectives if this strategy isn't implemented.

This strategy addressed the major constraint that has prevented the company from improving costs. This strategy addresses the key area we have targeted for cutting costs. We must meet this target as management has determined that competition will be lowering its costs 15 percent per year.

Creating a Strategic Advantage

Strategic advantage strategies should be bold and produce more growth than the company's objectives.

Higher management wants to hear: The strategy offers a platform not just for the next three years but for a much longer term.

We are the only company with enough projected revenue over the next two years to switch from batch to continuous production. That will give us a cost advantage that will allow us to gain market share and keep our competition from duplicating our strategy.

Action-oriented needs to hear: The implementation details have been worked out and the rewards of the strategy (meeting the growth objectives) will come quickly.

If the strategy is approved we can quickly move forward as the equipment required can be delivered in six weeks. Within three months we will begin meeting our interim objectives.

Analytical needs to hear: The strategy analysis was thorough; the program will meet or exceed the growth plans.

The strategic action plan will consume all our resources available to meet the internal changes required for our objectives. Since the resources won't be available to pursue another strategy, we analyzed this proposal from several perspectives and studied implementation at other companies before recommending it.

Conservative or hostile needs to hear: The strategy is clearly better than any other choice.

This strategy is key to the company meeting its growth objectives. If we choose to pass on this potential growth, we will fall behind competition, and we don't have another strategy to propose. This strategy is bold. It will meet our objectives, and we have great confidence that we can introduce this program.

Addressing New Opportunities

Higher management wants to hear: The company is following a leading edge opportunity.

This opportunity has just opened up because a leading supplier must be sold. Seizing this opportunity is a bold move that will control the majority of our material costs for at least two years, and put us far ahead of our corporate cost-cutting objectives.

Action-oriented needs to hear: This opportunity is a short-term window for which the company has the resources to immediately pursue.

We only have six weeks to act on this opportunity before our exclusive rights run out. We have the resources to move now, both financially and with workerpower, and moving now will meet our productivity goals for the next three years.

Analytical needs to hear: The opportunity has been evaluated against other opportunities that could also be pursued.

When I first became aware of the opportunity I felt it looked like a perfect solution to our growth goals. But before jumping on it, I created an evaluation chart to compare it against other opportunities and this one was far better than the rest in terms of results and ease of implementation.

Conservative or hostile needs to hear: The company needs to move ahead or it will be passing on a clear-cut path to meeting its objectives.

Strategically we must move on this opportunity. We may not find a better way to meet our objectives and we can't afford to have people think we contributed to delaying or preventing a winning path to our objectives.

Chapter 9

Add Value to Customers

Chapter 8 discussed how the strategy will provide growth to the company. The growth sometimes comes from increased operations, but in the end, all growth comes because you add more value to the customer. Substantial, long-term growth happens when you provide the values to customers that are important to them.

Malt-O-Meal makes generic cereals such as Toastie O's, a generic version of Cheerios. They sell the product at a generic price and have a nice business. That provides a benefit, but it doesn't get customers overly excited as they sell traditional tasting cereals that can be bought from others. Their only value is a cheaper price. Trader Joe's, on the other hand, sells a line of gourmet cereals that taste great with many flavors and textures. This adds value to the customers in what they feel is most important: great taste. Trader Joe's cereals are also cheaper than similar brands from the major cereal companies, but they are cheaper in the "best tasting cereals" category. Adding value in an important area makes Trader Joe's a much stronger company with higher growth than Malt-O-Meal, who has just modest growth every year.

External Strategies

External strategies are more easily tied to customers' needs, but you want to go one step beyond this and show that you are offering something very important to the customer.

Solving a Problem

Higher management wants to hear: The solution as implemented meets an important customer concern, desire, or need.

We've been able to tweak our strategy so it doesn't just solve the problem, but it also improves the (state a specific benefit) that our customers tell us is the most important reason they buy from us.

Action-oriented needs to hear: The customer will recognize immediately the value the company is offering.

Before suggesting this strategy, we looked at past customer surveys on what areas the customers would like to see us improve. We were able to solve our problem in a way that also addresses one of our customers' top three suggestions (name the suggestion). Customers will notice the improvement immediately, and this strategy allows us to turn a bad situation into our advantage.

Analytical needs to hear: The proposed value has been well documented in interviews with customers.

We have taken in data on customers' priorities for years, but we haven't always cataloged them in an efficient manner. If we receive support for our strategy our first step will be to e-mail a group of 100 customers to get their feedback on whether we are targeting a customer hot button with this strategy.

Conservative or hostile needs to hear: We can't afford to pass on this strategy; it is too important to customers.

New equipment is coming on the market, and our current equipment can't be counted on to interact with it efficiently and accomplish what customers want. We can solve this problem and also add two new features that target customers' top needs. If we don't do this, another company might, and then we could see our customer base erode.

Improving Performance

Higher management wants to hear: Our improved process also allows us to better meet our customers' future desires.

This improvement of our performance also targets an important customer goal that has been raised repeatedly in customer interviews: it offers an easier way to customize the final product that the customer buys.

Action-oriented needs to hear: Customers will easily grasp why the improvement adds customer value.

The beauty of this improvement in our performance is that our customers will immediately understand that we meet their number one desire better than any other competitor.

Analytical needs to hear: The company is certain that the improvement will be perceived by customers as one that adds value to them.

This strategy provides increased functionality that customers greatly value. We interviewed customers at one of our local dealers for three days. Every one of the customers rated the improvement at 7 or higher on a scale of 1 to 10 as being important to them.

Conservative or hostile needs to hear: Customers are enthusiastic.

We considered five improvements before recommending this one. Our choice was easy as it was our customers' enthusiastic first choice.

Creating a Strategic Advantage

Higher management wants to hear: The advantage will provide value to customers for an extended period.

Using this technology on an exclusive basis will produce an improved performance that meets the government-mandated performance goals for the next five years. Customers won't need to worry about buying new, or retrofitting their equipment for a minimum of five years. That provides tremendous value to our customers.

Action-oriented needs to hear: The new advantage will be an easy sell to customers because of the perceived advantage.

Our breakthrough screen technology offers a user interface that is so customer friendly that customers need less than 30 minutes of training. This is compared to over three hours for our competition. One trial run and customers are sold.

Analytical needs to hear: The argument that the strategy provides value to the customers is backed up with customer feedback.

We want to ensure that the strategy maximizes value for the customer. We have involved input from over 20 customers prior to creating the strategy. They back the strategy 100 percent and have all promised to increase business with us once we complete our implementation.

Conservative or hostile needs to hear: Key customers are supportive of this strategy.

The three customers that the management team listens to, (name the three), have all come out in favor of this strategy. They will offer management an earful of negative reviews if we fail to move ahead.

Addressing New Opportunities

Higher management wants to hear: This opportunity ties into customers' priority goals.

Our customers want to be able to better serve this new application for their products. Adding this new service will allow our customers to offer a better package to their customers.

Action-oriented needs to hear: Customers will quickly see the value to them if the company pursues this opportunity.

Pursuing this opportunity provides us with a major selling point as it shows without a doubt that our major interest is meeting the key needs of our customers so that they can in turn grow their business.

Analytical needs to hear: The opportunity should be pursued because it provides more value than any other option the company has considered.

The strategy of capitalizing on this opportunity produces strong benefits to the company, but it also has the crucial advantage of providing increased value to the customer. Our studies indicate our customers will spend on average six hours less per month on their operations once we execute this strategy.

Conservative or hostile needs to hear: Customers want us to pursue this opportunity.

This opportunity provides the same benefits to customers as the opportunity we passed on last year. As you know we received many customer complaints after we failed to seize that opportunity. Customers will be very upset if we pass again on an opportunity that they perceive will better meet their objectives.

Internal Strategies

Companies make a major mistake when they feel internal strategies don't impact customers. Internal moves should also be made to improve your company's ability to meet your customers' current or future needs.

Solving a Problem

Higher management wants to hear: Solving the problem positions the company to meet an important customer need.

This solution goes beyond just solving a problem; it dramatically cuts our customers' administrative costs.

Action-oriented needs to hear: Customers will be excited; the solution provides extra value to the customer.

We will be able to create a real buzz with this solution because realigning our technical teams and assigning one team to each customer allows our customers for the first time to have an assigned team to understand their ongoing problems.

Analytical needs to hear: Customers will see the same value of the strategy as the company does.

One of the additional benefits to solving our packaging cost problem is that we are helping two of our customers minimize their packaging waste, a priority to both now that they have to pay to recycle.

Conservative or hostile needs to hear: Strategy needs to be implemented because the consensus is that the solution also meets a key customer need.

One of the reasons this solution has picked up steam in the organization is that it also gives our application engineering department more time to customize solutions to meet specific customer requirements. This is a customer benefit the company has been promising for over 18 months.

Improving Performance

Higher management wants to hear: The improvement provides a key function that helps the company satisfy customers' needs or demands.

Improving our inventory management system will allow us to fill expedited order requests over 50 percent of the time, which will help our customers deliver their orders on time.

Action-oriented needs to hear: The company will be able to sell this new benefit to customers and increase sales.

This improvement in our internal customer service operations will allow customer service reps to give an update on shipping in seconds. This will immediately help customers improve their production scheduling and move closer to a lean production system.

Analytical needs to hear: The extent of the value to the customer has been evaluated.

This improvement in our database system also provides a key customer benefit: It allows them to quickly obtain the right repair information from customer service. Our research with customers indicates that their obtaining key information in a timely manner will cut their service costs 10 percent.

Conservative or hostile needs to hear: The increase in value to the customer is even more important than the impact on internal operations.

This improvement in the quality department will allow customers to cut their inspection time by 50 percent as our product uniformity will improve dramatically. The customers' savings will be even greater than ours.

Creating a Strategic Advantage

Higher management wants to hear: The advantage resulting from this internal strategy will result in major market share growth.

Our strategy of distributing our technical analysis team at regional offices will offer those offices the research they need to recommend stocks and provide major customers a perspective on their local stocks. Being the first of the national brokerages with this strategy will be a huge advantage to our sales force as customers like to invest in key local stocks.

Action-oriented needs to hear: The success of this strategy is crystal clear; executing the program will not present any major problems.

Signing this agreement which aligns our research staff and research projects with the university will give us access to the nation's most successful development program in our field. This move will make us the market leader in under two months. Key customers will want to see our salespeople frequently to learn what's coming in the market.

Analytical needs to hear: The analysis of how customers will value this strategy was thorough.

I believe this strategy offers value to kitchen designer customers as it allows them to access an easy-to-navigate photo retrieval and product specification site. We had six designers take a three-day "test drive" of the system and all rated it a 9 or 10 on a scale of 1 to 10.

Conservative or hostile needs to hear: The presenters have far more and far better information than he or she has.

This strategy will cut our costs and improve our operations a minimum of 15 percent, and at the same time generate value to the customers by allowing us to stage our shipments so the customer can cut project assembly and completion time by 50 percent. I've completed a financial analysis, an implementation plan, a risk-reward study, and a report on my conversations with customers. The reports all demonstrate that we should move forward.

Addressing New Opportunities

Higher management wants to hear: The opportunity helps the company, helps the customer, and improves the company's image.

Using this new part numbering and database system will help us gain ISO certification which helps our ISO customers keep their certifications. It will also allow us to electronically transfer serial and part numbers, along with product configuration details that can automatically be loaded into the customers' database. The customer will have less entry time and more accurate records.

Action-oriented needs to hear: Customers will understand and appreciate the value the company will be offering them.

This improved data tracking will allow us to offer customers 90-day price protection on all quotes, three times the industry norm of 30 days. That is an important benefit when the economy is slow and customers need to wait until they have cash in hand to order.

Analytical needs to hear: All of the downside risks have been carefully evaluated.

The upside of this strategy is the customer can generate its financial reports only hours after having their financial data complete. If the strategy doesn't work, and we are late, customers will be irate. We've ensured that every major component has extensive field experience, and we will send two of our people for five weeks of training at a company that has already taken advantage of this new process flow for high-speed printing.

Conservative or hostile needs to hear: The company has a lot to gain; introduction will not be difficult or expensive compared to the strategy's benefits.

The value to the customer of this change is about 20 percent of whatever that customer purchases in a year. We save 5 percent or more on our operations. Our team of four will have this strategy up and running and benefitting everyone, the company and our customers, inside of two months.

Chapter 10

Detail the Costs

Now that you have worked hard to show why your strategy offers an ideal platform to provide the company growth and offer the customer value, you need to deal with the issue of cost. Your strategy will have a cost, which you should state specifically, but then you need to explain how the costs will be paid, and, if appropriate, what impact paying those costs will have on other company programs. The costs should be stated as money and, if relevant and significant, also list the number of employees or other resources needed to implement the strategy.

External Strategies

Solving a Problem

Higher management wants to hear: The costs are justified by the benefits; well within budget guidelines.

The costs of this program are (state $ amount), plus we will tie up two process engineers for 30 days each. The problem will cost us far more than that if it lingers over the next six months and we can use funds from our maintenance budget to pay the costs.

Action-oriented needs to hear: The costs won't affect, or will minimally affect, implementation of other programs.

The costs will be under $15,000. We are under budget on our outsourced administration budget and we can use those funds to pay for the program and avoid delaying any other strategies.

Analytical needs to hear: The program has been evaluated against other choices and offers the best cost-benefit ratio.

The cost of this strategy is $26,000. We have the money available in the marketing budget to cover this cost. This strategy had a better cost-benefit ratio than the other proposed solutions, and it also is the only one that we could pay for without major restructuring of this year's budget.

Conservative or hostile needs to hear: We can't afford to pass on this strategy; it is too important to customers.

The cost is projected to be $38,500. Despite the cost we need to move ahead because the situation is creating additional problems that could cost us several distributors. We will need to hold back on our field service training programs for three months to pay for the program.

Improving Performance

Higher management wants to hear: Costs are far less than the benefits; results in a favorable variance to budget.

The cost of this program is $125,000. We will recoup this cost in four months with increased sales in the Northeast region and at the end of the year we will be ahead of budget.

Action-oriented needs to hear: The costs are well defined and won't be higher than anticipated.

The $48,750 cost is well documented with quotes from our vendors. We will be able to offset these costs with a realignment of our trade show attendance this fall.

Analytical needs to hear: Costs have been evaluated by a qualified individual or team.

The accounting department has determined the cost of the strategy to be $22,500. We will cover the costs by cutting back on our ad program the last three months of the year and by delaying our new brochure for three months.

Conservative or hostile needs to hear: Cost is low compared to the benefit; can't afford to pass on this opportunity.

The $24,000 cost is low compared to the $250,000-plus in sales we will gain for the year. We can't afford to pass on this improvement as it positions us to land several of the market's top 10 customers.

Creating a Strategic Advantage

Higher management wants to hear: The cost creates a strong advantage comparable to or better than other programs in the past.

This program will cost $425,000 to implement over the next 18 months including the time of current employees, adding two new employees, plus all associated costs. This program will increase our market share of our major market at least two points and will cost only 50 percent of our last major program. We currently have a $125,000 positive variance on administrative and marketing costs that we will use to start the program, and we will also cut $125,000 from the marketing and administration budget from the remainder of the year to launch the program. We will cover the remainder of the $425,000 with our increased sales and we will end the year on budget.

Action-oriented needs to hear: The costs can be absorbed or covered without negatively affecting any department.

The costs are significant but we can cover the $98,000 in costs from the 5 percent higher margins we will obtain due to higher prices. Costs will be placed against quality control and factory overhead, but the higher margins will keep the plant at its budgeted cost of goods sold.

Analytical needs to hear: All costs have been considered, including opportunity and personnel costs when evaluating the strategy.

The cost of the program will be $418,000. This is a complete cost, including current personnel, one new hire, equipment, software, and travel and marketing costs. This program also will prevent us from pursuing an alternate market, where we were projecting annual sales of $500,000 to $1 million. We will pay for this program from the budget for the Licensing Agreement program that we have dropped.

Conservative or hostile needs to hear: Costs are high, but it is the only cost-effective strategy to meet the company's objectives.

The costs of the program are $1.2 million over the next year. The company has budgeted $1.75 million for reorganizing its distribution network. This amount will cover the cost of the strategy. There are only two other proposals for reorganization, and neither of those has as high a cost-benefit ratio, and both have higher cost.

Addressing New Opportunities

Higher management wants to hear: The cost is quite reasonable considering the size of the opportunity.

The cost to this program will be $375,000. The market size is over $10 million and we should be able to at least gain 25 percent market share. We will drop our efforts to pursue the budgeted market opportunity (state what it is) to cover the cost of the program. This opportunity is four times bigger than the budgeted market opportunity.

Action-oriented needs to hear: The costs of the program will not adversely impact operating margins of the division or the company.

The costs to go after this opportunity are $285,000, which includes new personnel, a new marketing program, and changes in our trade show booth. Pursuing this opportunity will enhance the sales in particular of our Advantage line so we are going to cut that line's marketing and trade show budget to pay for the introduction.

Analytical needs to hear: The costs are an accurate reflection of what the company can expect.

Our costs have been projected by the marketing financial analyst to be $330,000. That covers all expenses. We will pay for the program with the budgeted money for the introduction of the E–2000 line, as that product has run into reliability problems in field tests.

Conservative or hostile needs to hear: No other programs have a cost-benefit ratio better than this proposal.

The program will cost $85,000, but it will make us a player in a $5 million market. This is the only opportunity available with a low cost with such a strong upside potential. We will delay our plant maintenance overhaul two months to introduce the program, and then use initial profits from the strategy to pay for the budgeted maintenance.

Internal Strategies

Solving a Problem

Higher management wants to hear: Costs are for a significant improvement, not simply to fund a program that is just enough to eliminate a problem.

The costs of the program are $95,000. But this strategy does not just solve our immediate problem; it is also putting in place several procedures that we had planned on adding next year. We can pay for the improvement from our budget line of IT maintenance and accounting software.

Action-oriented needs to hear: The solution won't disrupt overall operations; the solution will provide clear-cut benefits.

Our solution will cost $48,000. It solves the problem and provides additional benefits that are important to our quality certification. We can pay for the project from the money we had budgeted for quality certification, but we will also recover about twice the costs in savings.

Analytical needs to hear: Costs have been carefully calculated; cost impacts to other departments have been considered.

A detailed costing of this strategy projects the cost at $85,000. The solution can be paid for out of the affected department's budget and there will not be a cost impact on any other department.

Conservative or hostile needs to hear: Costs are in line with other solutions implemented in the past; strategy offers customer benefits.

The cost is $125,000 which is 10 to 20 percent lower than our solutions to similar problems in the past. We are losing over $25,000 a month now, and this solution will stop that hemorrhaging. The new solution will also save us $15,000 per month over our original budgeted costs. We will be unfavorable in our maintenance budget with the solution but will cut the deficit to $30,000 by the end of the year.

Improving Performance

Higher management wants to hear: The cost of the improvement can be justified by the company's improved ability to serve customers.

The planned improvement costs $275,000. It will cut our lead time by 40 percent, cut scrap, and also improve our quality. The project has a two-year payback based on scrap alone, but it has the added benefit of improving our customer service. This project will be paid for out of our capital equipment budget.

Action-oriented needs to hear: Costs are acceptable because customers will quickly notice their benefits from the strategy.

The cost of improving our order entry and billing system is $82,500. Money for customer service improvements has been budgeted and will cover the costs of this program. The new order entry system will drastically cut our 4 percent error rate on order entry and eliminate 99 percent of the billing errors we've made in the past. Our distributor customers will notice our "error free rate" within 30 days.

Analytical needs to hear: The cost provides a better cost-benefit ratio than other potential programs.

The cost of this administrative improvement is $50,000, but it will allow us to expand the work 30 percent without hiring additional personnel. We evaluated four improvements and this strategy had by far the best cost-benefit ratio. Besides our savings, customers will be able to get order shipment data online 24/7.

Conservative or hostile needs to hear: Costs are best spent now; waiting will be a mistake.

Enlarging the shipping area is a $75,000 expense, but it will allow us to get every shipment out in one day. We need to make this change now and improve customer service before our competitors' new plant comes online.

Creating a Strategic Advantage

Higher management wants to hear: Costs versus risk versus benefits: Does the program really make sense?

The cost is $450,000 to put in equipment that allows us to customize our product for each customer. Sixteen percent of our customers have requested a custom design at one time, and adding this equipment could raise sales $2.5 million, or 8 percent per year. We do have the money for the projected costs available in our capital budget that isn't currently earmarked for an immediate project.

Action-oriented needs to hear: The strategy has a high chance of success; cost is justified by the scope of the program.

The cost is $1.7 million, but it moves our production to the level where we can be considered for a large contract from a truck manufacturer. We would be one of only three companies in the market with enough volume to serve truck manufacturers. Landing just one of those customers would triple our sales. Without this expansion, the industry won't have the capacity required to serve customers' demands.

Analytical needs to hear: Costs of implementation, savings, and customer response have all been carefully evaluated.

The cost of $225,000, and savings of $515,000 per year, has been vetted by accounting, engineering, and an independent consultant. Marketing has interviewed 12 customers to verify demand. We are confident of all the numbers we are projecting for this program.

Conservative or hostile needs to hear: The cost is necessary as the company needs to reinvent its operations or move to the next state of business development.

The program will cost $1.5 million. We need to move ahead. The market is changing rapidly from a series of small customers to a market dominated by three major customers, which will increase the market by 500 percent. If we don't move forward, and establish ourselves first as the major supplier, we will definitely be left behind.

Addressing New Opportunities

Higher management wants to hear: The cost is justified because it is an important opportunity.

This technology will cost $65,000 to implement throughout the company's branches. This technology costs 50 percent less than the new IT system we were going to introduce and it provides more capabilities and a much better Web interface for customers.

Action-oriented needs to hear: The cost of the opportunity is reasonable; the company can move on the opportunity immediately.

Adding software to facilitate our work flow process will cost $82,000. This will eliminate the need for two people in production planning and we can implement the program in four weeks. We will fund the program by not replacing the software programmer who recently left the company.

Analytical needs to hear: Costs and benefits to the company are well researched.

Adopting the new advanced version of the optical inspection system will cost $40,000. With this system we will be able to demonstrate our materials have the lowest standard deviation in the industry. We successfully illustrated particle size analysis of ours and our competitors' product with two of our top customers and both were surprised at our tighter control of particle size.

Conservative or hostile needs to hear: Company may start to lag behind competition if this opportunity is not addressed.

This new smart technology that allows machines to wirelessly pass data without going through a server will cut production costs over 10 percent by allowing us to break away from sequential manufacturing. The benefits are so strong we have to expect competitors to adopt the technology. We need to move now to stay ahead of our competition.

Chapter 11

Making Money

In the end it is all about making money. A business is just like an investor, they have lots of choices and they should choose the option that offers them the highest return that has an acceptable risk. Money includes the "costs" part of the strategy that I discussed in the last chapter. But now is when you want to end the "delivering the power" part of your presentation about the money the company will be making (or losing) from the decision. You should have a positive money result to report before presenting a strategy. You can present the money part of the presentation as a return on investment (ROI), over one or more years; as a payback period, how long it will take to pay back the expense; or in terms of increased revenue and profit per year. Or you can present the money section with all three.

You can talk about money on a short-term, mid-term, or long-term basis, but you need to quantify, at least in ballpark terms, what the company will receive back. Money comes in many colors—revenue and its subsequent profits and costs are the obvious first two—but your strategy can also help you sell complementary products, solidify sales in an application or market to increase future sales, or allow you to add more production capacity without significant costs.

Start out all of your phrases with something similar to "the financials on this strategy look very strong."

External Strategies

Solving a Problem

Higher management wants to hear: The strategy provides a profitable return with additional side benefits.

We will have a payback period on our costs of just four months by recovering our lost sales. In addition, we feel solidifying our position at our major customers should increase sales of other products (state the amount) in the first year, with gross margins of (state the amount).

Action-oriented needs to hear: The financials indicate the company should move ahead immediately.

This strategy will bring us back to 10 percent over budgeted sales and profit levels for the year. Just the increase in sales produces enough profit for a payback period of less than six months, plus our margins will increase 2 percent. Our financials exceed the company spending guidelines for new programs by over 50 percent.

Analytical needs to hear: The financial data is accurate; this strategy is the best option.

The financial data that we have prepared with accounting shows an ROI of 80 percent per year for the next three years. None of the other three proposals being offered

promise any results except stemming the sales losses we
have suffered.

Conservative or hostile needs to hear: Everyone will be
pleased with the financials.

This strategy dramatically turns our problem into a profit
opportunity. We will be able to produce a three-month
payback period by resolving the problems of the product
auction Web site with increased advertising. We also
expect to increase sales of our services on the site by
15 percent, increasing annual profits a minimum of (state
amount). The results are far better than anyone expected
when the problem first came to light and we have received
enthusiastic support from all the field managers.

Improving Performance

Higher management wants to hear: The project has great
returns with low risk.

The project has a 25 percent return on its investment. We
feel the return numbers are solid with little risks because
our two major distributors have both reported that, with
these improvements, they will be able to increase
business with us.

Action-oriented needs to hear: Good returns; improvements
can be in place quickly; project has side benefits.

This project will have a one-year payback period and we
can start initiating phase one in three weeks. This
improvement will also help position us as a player in the
manufacturing software market which will help pave the
way when we introduce our two new products next year.

Analytical needs to hear: There has been an in-depth analysis on the financials; risks have been appropriately considered.

The financial analysis we've done with our consulting group shows a 37 percent ROI for the first three years. We also did an analysis for scenarios where our two biggest risks occur: (state what those risks are). The first risk developing would give us an ROI of 22 percent while if the second risk occurs, our ROI would only drop to 30 percent.

Conservative or hostile needs to hear: Financial ratios are positive; company needs to move ahead.

This improvement will increase sales 15 percent, and profit 24 percent, over the next three years. Our return on investment will be 41 percent. More importantly we have not changed our product line for this application in four years. Our competitors have upgraded every two years and without this improvement we could find ourselves out of the market.

Creating a Strategic Advantage

Higher management wants to hear: The strategy has a strong ROI; additional benefits in the future.

This strategy has a projected annual ROI of 41 percent over the next five years on our current product line. At a minimum, the advantage also will increase sales of our upcoming Slim Line product line by 40 percent, and it will help the sales of our subsidiary in Europe by 25 percent.

Action-oriented needs to hear: The strategy has a strong ROI; plan is ready to be implemented.

We will have an 18-month payback period. We have an implementation plan ready to put into place and can have the project ready to present to customers in six months.

Analytical needs to hear: This strategy has been evaluated against others.

Our ROI for this project over the next three years is 55 percent. We also evaluated two other strategies that held similar high returns. We chose this strategy because it provides an advantage that is most important in our market's fastest growing application (state the advantage).

Conservative or hostile needs to hear: No other project is available; ROI equivalent to past successful projects; company will lag behind competition if it fails to reinvent itself.

Our ROI at 38 percent on this strategy is higher than both of the company's last two initiatives (state what they are). Those two initiatives have carried us for three years but we need a new program to keep our momentum. This strategy is strong, with a good return. We don't have another strategy to substitute for it.

Addressing New Opportunities

Higher management wants to hear: The strategy has a strong ROI; reasons opportunities will present strong margins.

We have a nine-month payback period on this opportunity. Our partner in this market has always had margins over 50 percent, and our combined marketing efforts are targeted at high end consumers who typically buy high margin products.

Action-oriented needs to hear: The strategy has strong financials; opportunity can be quickly pursued; no major obstacles in sight.

All of the financial ratios on this project are 50 percent higher than our minimum thresholds. We have a full rollout plan ready for release, and none of our competitors has taken any steps to pursue this opportunity.

Analytical needs to hear: Plan has a high return on investment; information that supports that the opportunity is real.

We are projecting a 41 percent ROI, the highest ROI we have generated on a major project in the last three years. This is based, in part, on the fact that the market size of this opportunity is expected to grow 40 percent per year over the next three years. This growth is supported by the Association of National Retailers, the Distributor Council, and our own internal market surveys.

Conservative or hostile needs to hear: Margins are good; pursuing this opportunity is a "can't miss" proposition.

The margins for products targeted at this opportunity are 8 percent higher than our standard margin. We already have three technology companies ready to adopt our software and we will surpass all of our company goals if we only get those three companies as customers.

Internal Strategies

When it comes to internal strategies, most people only look at costs and savings. But you should also add to the money equation what impact the strategy will have on customers, typically by increasing their orders to you.

Solving a Problem

Higher management wants to hear: The strategy has a strong ROI; funding for the program is available, preferably within budget guidelines.

This project has a six-month payback. Solving the problem with this strategy also puts us halfway to meeting the objective of adding a customized ordering page on our Web site for each customer.

Action-oriented needs to hear: Funding can be accessed now.

The project has a four-month payback time. By moving now, we can also cut our shipment time by 25 percent.

Analytical needs to hear: The project's returns are better than alternative uses of the money.

The problem is costing us (state amount) per month. The strategy will reverse those losses in two months with a four-month payback. Not one of the IT departments' other pending programs has a return of less than 12 months.

Conservative or hostile needs to hear: The strategy financials are strong; not moving forward will be a poor decision.

This strategy has a ROI of 75 percent and it solves a problem that may hurt our customer service in the near future. There is no reason to not move forward.

Improving Performance

Higher management wants to hear: The strategy ROI is strong; improvements will offer customer benefits.

This improvement has double the payback of our corporate guidelines. It fits into our long-term goal of implementing a lean manufacturing system that will allow us to offer "just in time" inventory shipment to our top customers.

Action-oriented needs to hear: The plan's financials are positive; the improvement's benefits will impact customers quickly.

We will have a 58 percent ROI on this productivity improvement. It will allow us to undercut the competition's pricing and increase our capacity by 30 percent to be able to meet the market's expected rapid expansion.

Analytical needs to hear: Improvement is significant and the difference will be noticed.

This improvement has a 15-month payback period, and will offer even better returns in the future because it radically improves the company's quality, reducing scrap. The improved quality also puts us in a strong position to pick up automotive accounts.

Conservative or hostile needs to hear: The plan financials are so strong that no one will be willing to stand in the way of the project.

Our ROI this year will be 42 percent, and the ROI next year will be 100 percent. These are better ROIs than we have ever had on a project, and in addition the project will let us bid on big projects from two new prospects, which could add 20 percent to our revenues.

Creating a Strategic Advantage

Creating a strategic advantage typically creates high costs and low ROI in the first year or two, but then a high ROI in years three through five. Typically you need to explain ROI over more years with a strategic advantage strategy. Again tie the advantage into customer benefits whenever possible.

Higher management wants to hear: The ROI will be positive at the beginning, and very high in years three to five; fits with company overall efforts.

The new ceramic firing equipment meets our long-term goal of being able to offer a unique high-end line of products for department stores. Year two we will have an ROI of 10 percent, but it will rise to 30 percent in year three and 60 percent in year five.

Action-oriented needs to hear: The plan has strong financials; high chance of success; and strong support within the company.

The ROI averages 38 percent over the next five years. This advantage has been created by our R&D department with the help of two universities and targets a large unmet market need. We can move for quick implementation as most, if not all, of the mid-level managers are in favor of executing this strategy.

Analytical needs to hear: A long-term market situation dictates pursuing the advantage; it has been well researched.

Our ROI over the next three years will be 40 percent. The market change this strategy addresses is dictated by new research that was supported by six university papers at the last industry conference. Reports have been filed by leading consultants indicating the market change is real.

Conservative or hostile needs to hear: The financials are good; the company must move ahead with the times or fall behind.

We have excellent ROI on this project, 44 percent over the next five years. This is 10 percent higher than our strategies implemented three years ago and five years ago. We need this strategy to avoid tying the hands of our marketing and engineering departments in their introductions of new products targeted at specific customer needs.

Addressing New Opportunities

Higher management wants to hear: The financials are strong; strategy fits into the company's growth goals.

Adopting this process change has a payback period of 12 months, and will increase profits 10 percent per year for the next four years. The strategy will smooth out the production flow and help the company branch out of its exclusively high-end markets into the mid-priced department store market.

Action-oriented needs to hear: Financials are strong; money is available now; an action plan is ready.

This strategy's ROI at 45 percent is 10 percent over the company minimum's goals. We can pay for this added improvement because we can use this new technology to fix the (state the exact problem) without spending any additional money than was originally budgeted. Our action plan is ready and we can start execution within 30 days.

Analytical needs to hear: Plan has strong financials; improvement will be sufficient for three-plus years.

The five-year average annual return on investment will be 64 percent. According to our studies, and a study by an outside consultant, this improvement should have a life of four to five years before the next upgrade will be required.

Conservative or hostile needs to hear: The ROI on this project stands heads and shoulders above any other option.

This strategy has an 18-month payback and will raise our margins 4 percentage points. We have identified in our three-year plan four projects, not one of which has financials that come close to this one.

Part Three

Closing Out: Getting Commitments

In Part One I discussed making listeners comfortable; minimizing their skepticism. Part Two covers delivering the power behind the strategy, explaining why the strategy is right in terms of money, and preparing the company for the future. In this section we close out the presentation by getting commitments. This involves: explaining the key elements of the program so that people will understand you can execute the strategy; detailing the advantages to reinforce the need to move ahead; and finally asking for action. You will not always be asking for a go-ahead for the program. Your presentation might be to someone whose support you need before presenting to top management, or you might need the go-ahead to prepare a final action plan or need some other intermediate step. What counts is that you get a commitment to keep the project moving forward.

Chapter 12

Explain the Key Tasks

I've seen many otherwise great presentations ruined at this phase. Some presenters want to show how thoroughly they have prepared and end up having a key elements section turn into a complete action plan, which convinces people the project will be difficult to implement. Or the presentation is so long it cancels out all the earlier momentum. Another problem with presenting too much information is you invite too many comments and critiques that you may have to adopt into your strategy, or worse yet that will derail the whole effort. Your best bet is to keep your key tasks short, and try to keep your number of tasks down to four or less. Let your listeners trust you to complete the job. Building that trust has been one of the main purposes of the presentation up to this point.

This chapter deals with your opening phrase for the key tasks and what parts of a key task you should include. The parts of a key task that you might list are: a brief description; person or department responsible; and the timeline. For analytical people and conservative or hostile listeners you may also want to include the costs for the task and the funding source, even though you have talked about it earlier. Giving that detail shows the analytical people you have been thorough, and it lets conservative people know you've done your homework and that they will have trouble derailing your project.

For example, consider a project that will give a company more accurate cost data on its production. "The first task will be for the manufacturing engineering department to establish raw material usage for each manufactured part. The department can start compiling this data on May 1 and should have it completed by June 15th. Two engineers will work on the project 15 hours per week and we can complete the project within the normal payroll without any consulting help."

There will be times people come back and ask for a complete plan. If they do, just set a date for presenting that plan. Don't try to ad-lib your plan as you are unlikely to be effective.

After the opening statement, simply state "the first task will be" or "the key tasks are" and then list the specific tasks relevant to your project.

External Strategies

Solving a Problem

Higher management wants to hear: Execution of the strategy will be routine.

Parts to include: department or person involved; timeline.

The tasks are straightforward and divide nicely by departments.

Action-oriented needs to hear: The timeline is tight but can be executed.

Parts to include: department or person involved; timeline.

Our timeline to respond, based on market feedback, is no more than three months. We can execute the strategy in that time.

Analytical needs to hear: Details have all been considered.

Parts to include: department or person involved; timeline; cost for task; source for funding.

Every aspect of the plan has been looked at and all the required people identified.

Conservative or hostile needs to hear: Nothing is going to go wrong.

Parts to include: department or person involved; timeline; source of funding.

We've streamlined the work groups to expedite the process and avoid interdepartmental mix-ups.

Improving Performance

Higher management wants to hear: Sufficient resources can be recruited to execute the strategy.

Parts to include: department or person involved; timeline.

We have identified key people from each department plus one consulting firm to execute the strategy effectively.

Action-oriented needs to hear: The strategy will be implemented quickly.

Parts to include: department or person involved; timeline.

We need this project to start out with momentum so we have taken care to ensure that we have enough resources for a fast start.

Analytical needs to hear: Contingencies are in place to keep the project on schedule.

Parts to include: department or person involved; timeline; cost for task; source for funding.

We have identified our basic introduction team, plus department managers have pledged additional help if needed. We can also utilize as backup the consulting firm we used last year on our engineering design project if we fall behind.

Conservative or hostile needs to hear: There is no doubt the strategy can be successfully implemented.

Parts to include: department or person involved; timeline; source of funding.

This project is much simpler than our last improvement and we have the same resources employed to guarantee a successful implementation.

Creating a Strategic Advantage

Higher management wants to hear: The company's organization is being realigned as needed to guarantee a successful launch.

Parts to include: department or person involved; timeline.

We've considered both workerpower and the company organization as this strategy has major resource commitments. Marketing has identified three people to head up this department, and engineering and accounting have committed one person. We will be able to stay with our current organization with just minor realignment.

Action-oriented needs to hear: The project is ready to move forward without any delays.

Parts to include: department or person involved; timeline.

Four departments will be involved in this introduction. Each has identified a lead person and support staff, and we expect to start implementation in 30 days and complete the project in seven months.

Analytical needs to hear: Rationale to support that there are enough resources to do the job.

Parts to include: department or person involved; timeline; cost for task; source for funding.

We will have a task force of six people from the three involved departments to execute this strategy. Our last major project (state what it was) proceeded successfully with a similar task force of six people so we are confident we have sufficient staff and funding in place.

Conservative or hostile needs to hear: The project will succeed without delaying any other important projects.

Parts to include: department or person involved; timeline; source of funding.

We have indentified the staff and resources needed to finish the project in nine months. I've also spoken with each department head to see if any major budgeted programs will need to be delayed. Each of them has figured out a way to complete each of their budgeted programs by the end of the year.

Addressing New Opportunities

Higher management wants to hear: The company can pursue this opportunity without disrupting important plans.

Parts to include: department or person involved; timeline.

With just a minor amount of juggling we will be able to devote sufficient resources to this project without impacting our other three major programs.

Action-oriented needs to hear: The company can move ahead quickly without changing other deadlines.

Parts to include: department or person involved; timeline.

We are ready to pursue this opportunity immediately and we can do that while still executing the plans to meet the company's other priorities.

Analytical needs to hear: The implementation plan will be sufficient to generate the promised revenue.

Parts to include: department or person involved; timeline; cost for task; source for funding.

We are counting on this opportunity for 10 percent of our growth this year. Each department head understands the importance of meeting that objective and they have assured me the resources they need are in place.

Conservative or hostile needs to hear: The plan is orderly, there are no hidden obstacles.

Parts to include: department or person involved; timeline; source of funding.

We can capitalize on this opportunity within the current operations of each department with just two new hires.

We have considered potential problems and have contingencies in place to handle any unforeseen developments.

Internal Strategies

External strategies require interacting with customers and the market and generally companies have a relatively easy time having people work together. Internal strategies often run into obstacles from turf battles as different departments work to protect their particular areas. With an internal strategy you need to list who is coordinating the program and who will be responsible for implementing the strategy.

Solving a Problem

Higher management wants to hear: The person in charge will resolve the problem according to plan.

Parts to include: department or person involved; timeline.

Our second most experienced application engineer, who has resolved five problems over the last three years, will coordinate the three departments involved to meet our deadline of six months.

Action-oriented needs to hear: The right team is in place to effectively implement the internal solution quickly.

Parts to include: department or person involved; timeline.

We have scheduled key individuals to work on this strategy for the next 30 days so it can be implemented quickly.

Analytical needs to hear: Implementation plans have been thorough.

Parts to include: department or person involved; timeline; cost for task; source for funding.

Two of our IT specialists will head up the project. They have already analyzed the situation and are committed to a three-week turnaround on the project. Their plans have been reviewed by our IT consulting firm also and they are confident the plan is sound.

Conservative or hostile needs to hear: Key resources are committed; every effort has been made to ensure the project will go smoothly.

Parts to include: department or person involved; timeline; source of funding.

The strategy is ready to implement. Two engineers have been assigned, they have sufficient money for the project, and they have already created an in-depth project flow chart to finish the project in five months.

Improving Performance

Higher management wants to hear: The project will be able to document the performance and cost savings.

Parts to include: department or person involved; timeline.

The project implementation will be six months. The teams from accounting and marketing have already started to document our current cost and volume throughput and they will complete a final report to demonstrate our actual savings. The team is committed to delivering both the timetable and the final savings.

Action-oriented needs to hear: Improvements will go in place without any problems.

Parts to include: department or person involved; timeline.

The project will be completed in four months. Two members of the team have attended both a conference on implementing this improvement and visited another company in the area that implemented this improvement last year. We will be on schedule within our targeted costs.

Analytical needs to hear: The chosen implementation plan was the best choice.

Parts to include: department or person involved; timeline; cost for task; source for funding.

We will implement the improvement over the next nine months. Our plan was chosen from the three options presented to us by a consulting firm based on our follow-up calls with five companies that have already integrated this improvement into their operations.

Conservative or hostile needs to hear: The plan has enough research background and resources committed that it can't be attacked.

Parts to include: department or person involved; timeline; source of funding.

This improvement was part of the training course our engineers took last summer. At the course they spent a week at a company with this improvement in place. Their budget is based on the expenses actually incurred at that company.

Creating a Strategic Advantage

These will be major projects with inevitable problems in implementation. Reconfiguring a company's operations also has risk involved. The team leader is all-important for these projects.

Higher management wants to hear: An experienced person is in charge; an outline of required top management support; expected reports and updates.

Parts to include: department or person involved; timeline.

Our one-year timetable for the project is aggressive. (State individual's name) has agreed to lead our project and he or she successfully launched our last major reorganization in the plant. He or she has the support of the key managers. Once the project starts he or she will file weekly updates and have monthly meetings with a full update report.

Action-oriented needs to hear: The team is ready to go.

Parts to include: department or person involved; timeline.

The strategy's implementation has been evaluated by the team leaders, who have also visited other plants, had key vendors in, and discussed the final engineering with a consultant who has implemented this strategy two other times. The team is ready to proceed once the project is approved and is committed to completing the project within seven months.

Analytical needs to hear: The execution plan has been chosen because it offers the best balance of cost, ease of implementation, low risk, and likelihood of success.

Parts to include: department or person involved; timeline; cost for task; source for funding.

The implementation plan we are presenting was determined by input from other companies that have used this strategy and from multiple discussions with the involved engineering staff. This plan takes longer to implement at 12 months, but it causes less disruption and has lower costs.

Conservative or hostile needs to hear: The plan has no obvious holes to attack.

Parts to include: department or person involved; timeline; source of funding.

We are confident we can implement the key tasks I'll be reviewing next. We have had the plan reviewed by the two people (state their names) who led the last two major projects; we have visited the vendor who will supply the majority of the equipment; and we have the backup support of the Vice President of Operations.

Addressing New Opportunities

Higher management wants to hear: Execution will be successful; an orderly plan is in place.

Parts to include: department or person involved; timeline.

We are confident we can complete the tasks to take advantage of this new opportunity. We have already run some small-scale prototype work with success and have already resolved potential problems and have mapped out the introduction approach.

Action-oriented needs to hear: The implementation can move forward quickly.

Parts to include: department or person involved; timeline.

The completion of the tasks for this strategy has been agreed to by the parties involved and we expect to have the new equipment up and running in four months.

Analytical needs to hear: The plan to complete the tasks will be thoroughly evaluated before proceeding.

Parts to include: department or person involved; timeline; cost for task; source for funding.

We have a preliminary plan to complete the tasks involved with this strategy. Before we proceed we will have the plan vetted by additional personnel so we can ensure all contingencies are covered before we proceed.

Conservative or hostile needs to hear: The people involved in implementation have the qualifications to succeed; they are above reproach.

Parts to include: department or person involved; timeline; source of funding.

(State names) will be responsible for introducing this strategy. This will be their fourth time bringing new technology into our online ordering system. This improvement is less complicated than the others and they don't expect any delays in their work.

Chapter 13

Detail the Advantages

N ow that you've listed the key tasks that need to be completed, you should go back and give four to five advantages of the strategy. You don't need more than four or five, but they need to be strong. Normally you give the advantages in a bullet point list, one after the other. You want to reinforce those advantages now fairly close in the presentation to where you will ask for action.

The advantages you list should vary by the person you are presenting to. Higher management responds differently than an analytical person. Each phrase in the chapter explains what type of advantages that listener wants to hear, and then offers a perfect phrase you can use as a preamble prior to listing the advantages. After you state your phrase, then state "these are the strategy's main advantages" and then list them. Always be prepared to answer the question of what the disadvantages are, but don't include them in your presentation unless asked.

External Strategies

Solving a Problem

Higher management wants to hear: Strategy is a cost-effective, forward-thinking solution.

The approach we are recommending cost effectively solves our immediate problem but at the same time it fits into our long-term strategy of improving our market share in this key market.

Action-oriented needs to hear: The problem will be solved quickly before the market realizes it is a major problem.

Our major goal when we addressed the problem was to solve it before it became a lingering issue that the market would remember. This strategy accomplishes that goal.

Analytical needs to hear: This strategy is not a knee-jerk reaction to the problem.

There were several ways to approach this problem and we chose the strategy that offered the most significant advantages for the company.

Conservative or hostile needs to hear: The strategy is a consensus decision.

Our goal was to move quickly on solving the problem so we wanted to choose a strategy that we knew would have company-wide support.

Improving Performance

Higher management wants to hear: The program plays a significant part in the company's current business plan.

One of the advantages we wanted for this strategy was that it could play a significant part in meeting the goals stated in our three-year business plan. We feel this strategy does that as well as offers several other key advantages.

Action-oriented needs to hear: The strategy helps create market momentum.

One of the team's key goals in creating this strategy was to find one that included as an advantage a way to quickly start the company's market momentum. We chose this improvement and its implementation with that goal in mind.

Analytical needs to hear: Advantages are stronger than other possible approaches.

We considered pursuing several improvements but chose this one because it has stronger advantages than the other options.

Conservative or hostile needs to hear: Others in the company will respond well to this strategy.

This improvement in our online ordering system ties directly to a cornerstone of the company's philosophy: be "easy to do business with."

Creating a Strategic Advantage

Higher management wants to hear: This strategy meets, or goes a long way toward meeting, the company's future objectives.

The main goal when we began considering this plan was to create a strong strategic advantage that could carry the company toward its long-term growth objective. We feel we've been successful meeting that target.

Action-oriented needs to hear: Implementation will be straightforward with a low risk of significant delays.

The advantage of the program that was most important to us was that the market would continue to see the company moving forward more aggressively than any competitor. In addition to meeting those objectives the strategy also creates some significant other advantages.

Analytical needs to hear: Research has taken place to ensure the advantages are real.

Before presenting our strategy advantages to you, the team has conducted interviews with our sales force, key customers, and distributors to ensure that the market will prize these advantages.

Conservative or hostile needs to hear: The advantages tie in closely with the stated objectives of top management.

This strategy represents a major commitment by the company. We spent time making sure the advantages that we created are important to management, and that we could prove they would occur, if we were challenged.

Addressing New Opportunities

Higher management wants to hear: Pursuing this opportunity will improve the company's market position.

This new opportunity is the most significant one in the market today. A major advantage of this opportunity is that grabbing a leadership position in this new application will increase the company's market share and its importance to its distribution network.

Action-oriented needs to hear: Pursuing this opportunity will have a quick impact on the company's performance.

A key advantage of our strategy is that we can get it in place to start increasing sales and profits in the third and fourth quarters.

Analytical needs to hear: This is the best opportunity to pursue.

The market has several opportunities at the moment. We looked at the costs and benefits of each and felt the advantages of this opportunity were superior to any other choice.

Conservative or hostile needs to hear: The advantages of the new opportunity are too strong for the company to ignore.

This opportunity presents as strong if not stronger advantages of any other project I've seen presented over the past three years. This size opportunity comes up only once every three to five years, and our strategy to exploit the opportunity yields us tremendous advantages.

Internal Strategies

Solving a Problem

Higher management wants to hear: The solution fits into the company's future development plans.

The critical advantage we had to have on this solution is that it wouldn't impact or be impacted by the three-year plan on updating the IT department. The strategy also provides several other advantages.

Action-oriented needs to hear: The strategy allows for a quick, trouble-free implementation so the company can move on.

The company management wants the department to mature rapidly so we need our recommendation to offer the advantage of a quick turnaround.

Analytical needs to hear: The advantages are greater than other options.

We received input and solutions from others in the company and compared the advantages of each solution. This proposed strategy won hands down for the solution with the most and strongest advantages.

Conservative or hostile needs to hear: The advantages offered are important to key people in the company.

The one advantage management told us we had to deliver was the need for fewer operators. Besides delivering that key advantage this strategy offers several others.

Improving Performance

Higher management wants to hear: The improvement helps accelerate the company's internal goals.

The strategy has many advantages, but the most important one is it provides the first step in simplifying our server network. This is a vital step in meeting the company goal of unifying our technical service under one department.

Action-oriented needs to hear: The strategy is in a "ready-to-go state," the improvements will be noticeable immediately.

Among the strategy's advantages are that we have the people, money, and the equipment to start the project right away, and they have the experience to ensure we will see results within 60 days.

Analytical needs to hear: The expected results of this improvement will occur.

The program has four main advantages. These advantages related to improvement in performance have been documented in several test studies we have run at our other plant. That plant has also seen similar performance gains in their own operations.

Conservative or hostile needs to hear: The advantages will have strong support from others in the company.

We chose their strategy in part because the advantages fit into the major objectives of both our engineering and manufacturing groups, as well as the three-year objectives of the company's three productivity goals.

Creating a Strategic Advantage

Higher management wants to hear: The strategy either will complete or add significantly to the company's long-term growth and profit goals.

We felt in proposing a major program and commitment that the strategy had to deliver a significant contribution to the company's goal of cutting costs by 25 percent and increasing services to keep out foreign competition. We pursued this strategy because its main advantage cuts our cost by 20 percent, almost all of the total savings we require.

Action-oriented needs to hear: The team is ready to go, results will become apparent quickly.

One reason we are recommending this strategy is that we have the people in the company with the right skills to implement this project quickly, and with the skills to seamlessly introduce the strategy into current company operations.

Analytical needs to hear: Advantages have been weighed against the advantages of other potential programs.

Before recommending this strategy we did a careful analysis of three other programs that could have helped us meet the company's three-year targets. None of the other programs came close to helping the company meet its goals.

Conservative or hostile needs to hear: The program is the only one with sufficient advantages to meet the company's objectives.

This major program must deliver in significant ways for the company to withstand competition. No other strategy has these same strong advantages to give the design and cost advantages management wants.

Addressing New Opportunities

Higher management wants to hear: This opportunity has significant potential advantages to make the project worth pursuing.

This opportunity has a major advantage in that it can be introduced by just three people while having the potential to increase capabilities of the department by 20 percent.

Action-oriented needs to hear: Pursuing the opportunity doesn't present any significant challenges.

One advantage of the program is that our engineering group introduced this new technology twice before and they feel confident it can be introduced quickly without disrupting any of our operations.

Analytical needs to hear: The presenters can show the advantages will actually occur.

The advantages of the program have been checked out with the people who developed the software as well as through interviews with multiple users. We have also reviewed over 12 technical papers that study the effectiveness of the software.

Conservative or hostile needs to hear: Management in the company will prize these advantages.

We decided to pursue this opportunity after being charged by management to find a way to cut our direct labor hours. That is just one of the advantages of our strategy.

Chapter 14

Ask for Action

The end of your presentation should always be a call for action. There are many actions you might want. Sometimes you will just want someone's support for a presentation to higher management; other times you need approval to do a further study or to prepare an action plan; and of course, there are times when you want approval immediately. Make sure you know exactly what response you want to this question before you begin the presentation.

This chapter deals with phrases you can use to set up your call for action. After you state that phrase, you should follow-up the statement first with a statement about what you want and then a request for the person to agree. For example, "This strategy clearly fits into the company objective of rapid growth in targeted applications. (The perfect phrase.) I'm requesting today approval to prepare an implementation plan for introducing a new technical service feature, and then when that plan is complete, approval to move forward with the introduction. (The statement about the action you are looking for.) Do I have your approval to move forward?" (The request for agreement.)

External Strategies

Solving a Problem

Higher management wants to hear: The solution fits into the long-term strategies of the company.

This strategy works through our distribution network which ties closely into our three-year strategy of improving the effectiveness of our distributors.

Action-oriented needs to hear: The strategy is a solution that allows quick action that removes the problems.

This solution takes advantage of the workerpower we have in place to quickly eliminate the problem before it impacts our market share.

Analytical needs to hear: Strategy is clearly the best choice.

We graded this strategy much higher than any of our other options, and it provides a complete cost-effective approach to the problem.

Conservative or hostile needs to hear: Other parties will not complain.

The strategy meets the key goals of marketing, top management, and our distributors, and they should all strongly support this proposal.

Improving Performance

Higher management wants to hear: The improved performance is part of the company's long-term goals.

This strategy meets our important goal of introducing products with high durability to penetrate the road construction market.

Action-oriented needs to hear: The improvement will be introduced quickly and with enough impact to make the market notice.

We will be able to introduce this new improvement with a big splash at the industry trade show in October. It will be the highlight for our show marketing efforts.

Analytical needs to hear: Improvement is the best choice for the company to follow at this time.

None of the other improvements we could undertake matches this project's sales and growth potential with a similar modest cost. This program also has the fewest risks.

Conservative or hostile needs to hear: The project has a strong positive to negative ratio.

The project has a few potential problems but they are far outweighed by the positive aspects, including the strong sales growth the last half of the year.

Creating a Strategic Advantage

Higher management wants to hear: This strategy is aligned with the company's future objectives.

This advantage will increase sales 25 percent per year, and raise income 35 percent per year. Those are the objectives of our five-year strategic plan. The advantage is significant and it will take at least two years for competitors to respond.

Action-oriented needs to hear: Implementation will be straightforward and the market will perceive the advantage without an expensive or long-term marketing program.

The company can clearly implement this strategy as it plays to our major strengths. The strategy is also delivering benefits to the market that they have long wanted, and in a manner that is more effective than the market expects.

Analytical needs to hear: This project will succeed and produce the expected results.

We have been studying this strategy for over four months with a team from several departments and we are confident we will hit or exceed the introduction objectives and the three-year projected results.

Conservative or hostile needs to hear: The strategy is going to have support from top management.

This strategy came forward in a preliminary fashion last year and it had strong support from top management, though they had several concerns. We've addressed those concerns and are now confident we will have full support within the organization.

Addressing New Opportunities

Higher management wants to hear: This opportunity is significant and fits into the company's plan.

This opportunity is an offshoot of one of our markets targeted in our two-year plan. Exploiting this opportunity improves our position in the target market and increases our department's sales by 10 percent.

Action-oriented needs to hear: The company is positioned to capitalize on this opportunity quickly.

This opportunity is one our current sales and distribution staff can cover, and we only need to implement a new marketing program and attend an additional trade show. This will have a 5 percent positive impact on the bottom line this year.

Analytical needs to hear: This opportunity has been thoroughly studied.

We have received input from our sales department as well as three potential customers that this is indeed a viable strategy. This opportunity was a hot topic at the industry's last conference and we are confident it is the largest opportunity in the market today.

Conservative or hostile needs to hear: The company will look foolish if it fails to pursue this opportunity.

Our company has the equipment in place to exploit this opportunity faster than any of our competitors. Our top management has already been approached by customers stating the need for the company to move ahead. The company is going to look like it is dragging its heels if it is not the first to attack this new market.

Internal Strategies

Solving a Problem

Higher management wants to hear: The solution will expedite the company's current development plans.

The solution solves our problem by introducing early a key step in the company's lean manufacturing conversion plan. This strategy won't negatively impact the timing on that plan.

Action-oriented needs to hear: The solution won't interfere with the budgeted improvement plans already in place.

Our solution only calls for a minor change to the improvements already planned and it can be executed quickly.

Analytical needs to hear: The advantages are greater than other options.

Compared to our other options this solution has the best return, and it adds the most toward our planned operational upgrades.

Conservative or hostile needs to hear: The advantages offered are important to key people in the company.

The one advantage management told us we had to deliver with this strategy was the need for fewer operators. Besides delivering that key advantage, this strategy offers several other important advantages.

Improving Performance

Higher management wants to hear: The improvement will accelerate the company's internal goals.

This improvement ties directly into our operational improvement plan for next year, and will cut 20 percent off the time to introduce that plan.

Action-oriented needs to hear: The strategy won't disrupt company operations.

The consultant we are using will implement the plan with just one IT person's help and we can have the benefits of this improvement without any downtime.

Analytical needs to hear: The team has searched and removed any potential bottlenecks for the project.

We've had two team meetings where we considered what could go wrong with the project and have either minimized those possibilities or prepared a contingency plan for each. This project is ready to go.

Conservative or hostile needs to hear: The improvement is needed to keep the company up to date.

We haven't changed this part of our quality control section for four years and on plant tours customers have asked us when we will have an update in place. We need to move before we fall too far behind.

Creating a Strategic Advantage

Higher management wants to hear: This strategy delivers many if not all of the company's operational goals.

This strategy will let us deliver 90 percent of our operational goals inside of 15 months. That will free up management time to launch our needed expansion.

Action-oriented needs to hear: The benefits will be clear, and the strategy will motivate the affected employees.

The administrative group has struggled for consistency as it has had to outsource much of its work. This strategy will bring everything in house, cut our costs over 35 percent, and give total operational control to the administrative group. The administrative group now wants to push this program forward.

Analytical needs to hear: The strategy will deliver the promised benefits.

We understand the need to be sure this program delivers the benefits. We have run several analyses, had our other location's experts run an analysis, and checked on the benefits with other companies. We are confident the program will deliver.

Conservative or hostile needs to hear: The competitive advantage is a major step forward for the company; without it the company will struggle to meet its goals.

This strategy meets most of our near-term operational improvement goals. If we don't move on it, we will have to try and implement three to five programs to try and meet our objectives.

Addressing New Opportunities

Higher management wants to hear: Opportunity fits into the company's goals.

Adding this technology fits into our goal of having a better online quoting system. It meets not only our short-term needs but our three-year projected needs as well.

Action-oriented needs to hear: Pursuing the opportunity will build momentum in operations.

We can add this new technique in three months. It will meet our six-month operational improvement goals and give the department real momentum for hitting our annual cost-cutting target.

Analytical needs to hear: The introduction team is confident that the strategy can be executed as promised.

We have worked this project on a small scale in our model shop, and visited a company with the strategy in place. We have resolved a few problems but now the project is ready to go.

Conservative or hostile needs to hear: Opposition to the plan from others is unlikely.

Incorporating this new production planning is supported by the people we've spoken with, and it specifically targets key company goals. No one has voiced any concern about its implementation.

Part Four

Sample Presentations

The book has presented the fourteen key steps in presenting a business strategy. Each chapter stands alone and some readers may not feel comfortable in putting together each section into a final presentation. Other readers may not be convinced that this approach will lead to a strong strategy presentation. To address both possible reader concerns Chapter 15 and 16 offer eight sample strategy presentations. They demonstrate how the format fits together into a tight and powerful strategy presentation that will sell strategies to the listener.

One point to note is that the strategy presentation is not long, certainly not the hour or two presentations that are frequently prepared in many companies. Long presentaions have two drawbacks, they can obscure the strategy's straight forward reasons for moving ahead and they give the listeners many opportunities to find fault with some aspect of the presentation. This first presentation is to get the listeners to say "Yes." But if they need more information, then this presentation format allows them to say "Yes" this idea has merit, but I need some additional data. That allows you to then, typically at a later date, to offer that information and receive then ask again for approval to move forward.

Chapter 15

Sample Presentations: External Strategies

Presentation to Management—Create a Competitive Advantage

The Strategy

Form a division to serve senior dental patients that includes an advisory board of crown and bridge specialists and an alliance with leading dental schools.

Craft the Opening Statement

I believe the strategy I'll present today will offer the company a clear strategic advantage in one of our targeted customer groups, dental patients over the age of 55.

Show Careful Consideration

I've researched both this market from our internal data and from industry research available at the American Dental Association's office and at the University of Minnesota. I'm convinced we can show rapid sales growth in this target market if we create a product line strictly for senior patients.

Introduce the Strategy (Background Statement Plus Statement of Strategy)

Our malleable *dental crowns* and new products for taking impressions have been recognized by dentists as the best option for seniors, as they minimize the chances of creating new cracks in the tooth being reconstructed. My strategy proposal is to turn this into a strategic advantage by forming a senior patient division. This division will develop products and strategies based on the input of an advisory board of crown and bridge specialists. Those strategies will be modified and adjusted based on the marketing research and testing performed by certain leading dental schools who have agreed to be our alliance partners.

Address Listeners' Expected Concerns

This strategy will have a strong impact on our bottom line as it targets the market's fastest growing segment and the segment where we have our best margins. The strategy also will help our other product lines as it will help initiate sales to dentists who currently don't buy from us. Right now, the percentage of dentists we don't serve is 40 percent.

Show the Strategy as a Response

This strategy is a response to the fact that more and more seniors are keeping their teeth until they die and they keep seeing a dentist twice a year. Seniors' teeth are fragile but dentists highly recommend that seniors keep their teeth versus wearing dentures. Responding to this trend will help dentists and their patients as well as improve our bottom line.

Demonstrate a Good Fit

One reason I'm excited about this strategy is that it fits in with our corporate goal of being both a technological leader in the market and being the first company to respond to new opportunities that require dentists to use new products and procedures. We already have dental advisory groups and strong relationships with key universities on our other product lines and this strategy expands those relationships in a positive way.

Explain the Future Fit

The most important reason for moving ahead is that the market for senior dental services is expected to grow over 8 percent per year as the baby boomers continue to age. Baby boomers were raised with fluorinated water, have much better teeth than previous generations, and a large percentage are expected to keep up the dental visits until they die. We need to be positioned as the preferred supplier of products which meet the needs of this market.

Grow the Company

The strategy fits the market's future growth objectives and it also exceeds our three-year revenue growth goals of 10 percent per year. Our products sold to seniors make up 15 percent of our sales and we expect to double sales to this segment over the next three years. We are also projecting that we will be able to start supplying products to an additional 15 percent of the active dentists which will raise the sales of the rest of our product line.

Add Value to Customers

Besides helping ourselves, this new product line will have an enormous value to dentists. It helps prevent the dentists from accidentally breaking a tooth and more malleable products also provide a more pleasant experience for the patient. Breaking fragile teeth can occur, and most dentists then fix the tooth with a crown either for free or for a major discount. With a crown costing $1,000 and up, our new line could save dentists several thousand dollars per year.

Detail the Costs

This program will cost $525,000 over the next 18 months. That includes $75,000 to modify several products and change the packaging of the entire line, $75,000 for the dental advisory group, $150,000 to fund the university alliance research programs, and $225,000 for marketing. The program will be paid out of the marketing budget's usual operating funds. We are delaying the new literature package for our line of dental delivery units and delaying our ad campaign for our line of dental chairs to cover these costs.

Making Money

This strategy will have an annual ROI of 30 percent in year two rising to 50 percent in year four. We expect the strategy to raise sales 20 percent in year two and then add 10 percent per year in sales in years three, four, and five. This project has excellent returns and a strong sales increase for a relatively modest investment.

Explain the Key Tasks

This project will be led by the Marketing Director of our Crown and Bridge group. The product will be introduced in six months, including the product and packaging rollout, the dental advisory group, and the signing of university alliances. The key tasks for this project are:

1. Redesigning packaging and creating an ad program, which will be done by the marketing group.

2. Setting an advisory council of crown and bridge specialists which will be completed by our Regional Sales Directors.

3. Setting up university alliance partners and preparing and supervising research studies. This will be completed by the Director of our Dental Applications Staff who formerly was a professor at the University of Minnesota.

Detail the Advantages

The impetus behind this strategy was to develop a competitive advantage that could play a key role in meeting the company's three- and five-year plan sales goals. We also wanted to rely on the company's existing core strengths to do this. This is a quick summary of the advantages.

1. Utilizes core company technology that is already recognized as the market leader for treating senior patients.

2. Builds on the company's existing relationships with dentists and universities.

3. Targets the fastest growing segment in our market.

4. Provides the company a strategy that can be easily launched by people currently on staff.

5. Offers strong financials in every area: ROI, sales, and costs, and we can pay for the program out of our current budget.

Ask for Action

This strategy offers significant advantages for the company and can play a key role in meeting all of the company's growth goals. Today I'm requesting approval to move ahead with this project starting May 1. Do I have your approval to move forward?

Presentation to Action-Oriented People— Solve a Problem

The Strategy

Have Reliant Technologies, a manufacturer of products serving the same industry as the company, distribute the company's product in the Southeast.

Craft the Opening Statement

We are falling behind budget due to the disintegration of our Southeast distribution network. The strategy I'm proposing today will turn this situation around in six months and restore sales to last year's level.

Show Careful Consideration

There were several options and the proposal today is the result of conversations with our Regional Manager and our two key end users in the Southeast.

Introduce the Strategy (Background Statement Plus Statement of Strategy)

Our problem is that we've lost three distributors in the Southeast and our customers aren't getting the service they need and expect. Reliant Technologies is a regional company in the Southeast that makes a complementary product to ours, targeted at the same end user, that it distributes through its direct sales force. Reliant is willing to handle distribution of our product through its sales force.

Address Listeners' Expected Concerns

I believe this is the best solution to our situation both because it can be implemented quickly and because it will restore sales to prior levels.

Show the Strategy as a Response

One of the reasons we want to move quickly on this strategy is that we have had complaints from our two major end users in the Southeast.

Demonstrate a Good Fit

One of our key customers suggested this solution and it has the support of our Regional Managers. We shouldn't have trouble implementing the solution. Reliant also has sales and technical service people who have worked with our former distributors and so we will be able to train Reliant's staff quickly.

Explain the Future Fit

Long term, the company has a strategy of moving away from distributors and toward dealers who provide showrooms, training, and full-service backup. Distributors don't provide those services, and in fact rarely promote our product to new users. Reliant's salespeople do call on our customers and target customers, and we will be able to work with them to determine the training and sales material a dealer salesperson will need to successfully sell our product.

Grow the Company

Our first aim is to restore sales. Working with Reliant our Regional Sales Manager will be able to get our two best customers buying at previous levels, probably within 60 days. We also expect to see 100 to 200 percent sales growth in year two of this strategy. Reliant sells to three times more customers in the Southeast region than we do. Their regional focus has been a big asset for them in creating a dominant market position for its products in the Southeast. We expect that Reliant will start adding new customers in year two and expect to have a 10 to 20 percent growth rate in years three to five.

Add Value to Customers

Our customers in the Southeast will recognize immediately the advantage Reliant brings to them. They will benefit from a sales force with technical expertise, a strong customer service group, and our products being available to try out in Reliant's showrooms.

Detail the Costs

The costs of changing over to Reliant will be $85,000. That includes display products for the showroom, training of Reliant's sales force and technical service department, and modifying our Web page and marketing materials to list Reliant. The costs for this program can be absorbed by the East Coast region's sales budget.

Making Money

We expect to return to budget levels of sales in the Southeast region for this year, up from a drop of 55 percent, or $285,000. We expect an increase in sales over this year's budget of $500,000 next year, and a 10 percent increase overall. Our ROI for this strategy is over 100 percent in years two through five.

Explain the Key Tasks

We want Reliant to start selling our products in 60 days. To execute that we need to:

1. Negotiate an agreement. Our Contract Administrator and Regional Manager can start negotiations next week.
2. Train the sales and technical service staff. We can borrow sales staff from other regions and use half our technical service staff in a 30-day blitz to bring everyone up to speed.

3. Adapt our Web page, which we can do over the next two weeks.

4. Provide stickers on our literature for use in the Southeast region until we can reprint with Reliant's name listed as our Southeast Distribution outlet.

Detail the Advantages

If we can move right away we can resolve our problem before we totally lose our customer base in the Southeast. These are the main advantages of this program:

1. We will have our product sold by a well-respected company in the region.

2. We will immediately resolve our problems with our two biggest customers.

3. We will be implementing an early version of our dealer network so we can measure its success against our current distributor-based sales effort.

4. We stand to gain a significant increase in sales and profits for the region.

Ask for Action

We clearly need to move ahead quickly and decisively. I'm here today to ask your permission to move forward immediately. Are you ready to approve the program?

Presentation to Analytical People—Improve Performance

The Strategy

Add a new service, computer backup that will back up files automatically from people who work on the road or are traveling.

Craft the Opening Statement

We are a computer IT outsourcing service, primarily servicing small, to mid-size companies. The strategy I'm proposing offers those customers and prospects an important benefit that will increase our customer base.

Show Careful Consideration

We have interviewed 10 customers to see if this program would be of interest to them for a flat fee of $275 per month for up to 15 users, running up to $550 per month for 75 users. Three of the 10 stated they would probably add that service. If we have a 30 percent signup the project has a 15-month payback period.

Introduce the Strategy (Background Statement Plus Statement of Strategy)

Our customer base for our IT services has many small companies where a significant percentage of employees work at home or on the road. These professionals often work offline from their servers and there is a risk of their data being lost unless they have a system to regularly back up both the data on the server and on individual computers. I'm proposing we add a new service that backs up all of a company's computers three times per week for a monthly service fee.

Address Listeners' Expected Concerns

We have been looking at this strategy six months now. We have found three firms similar to the company who have successfully implemented the process in other markets. All three have indicated they are obtaining better than average margins on their sales.

Show the Strategy as a Response

We created this strategy because customers have told us that offsite personnel are not properly synchronizing their data on the server every night when they work offline. Many employees download a file and then work offline rather than online on the company server because their computer slows down when they are working on a file over the Internet. That creates problems when the files are not properly synchronized.

Demonstrate a Good Fit

This strategy will be easy to implement. Our IT director has evaluated the server requirements and staffing levels and feels we need an investment of $25,000 in hardware and one new IT specialist to execute the strategy.

Explain the Future Fit

This strategy also fits the company's long-term strategy of moving away from hourly billing and toward recurring revenue streams. We chose this strategy to move ahead on other product offerings because it produces additional high-margin revenue within six months while not requiring any major reorganization.

Grow the Company

This strategy contributes to our growth in two important ways: First, it raises revenue with our current customers—30 percent have indicated they will subscribe to the service. Second, the sales department also is committed to adding 10 to 15 percent new customers solely because of the new service. The sales department is projecting an overall sales increase of 30 percent if we adopt this strategy.

Add Value to Customers

The value to customers is that the service prevents different people from working on different versions of the same file. When that happens the files won't synchronize properly and all the work needs to be re-done. Customers indicate this can happen several times a month, and sometimes no one realizes the problem for several weeks. Avoiding one incidence of this a month would save the customers a minimum of $1,000.

Detail the Costs

Accounting and the IT department have put together a budget of $195,000 for the first 12 months. This includes equipment, the preparation of new sales materials, the training of the sales force, the hiring of an additional IT specialist, and the use of two additional staff IT specialists for three months to help set up and debug the program.

Making Money

We are expecting additional sales of $525,000 this year, and then $1.8 million next year. The service will have a 26 percent margin, a 15-month payback period, and in year two, our ROI will be over 200 percent.

Explain the Key Tasks

1. We have worked closely with the IT department head to ensure we meet our introduction deadline of 180 days. IT is prepared to add one or more specialists to the project if it falls behind schedule. The IT department head will be responsible for the project. These are the key tasks of the program: set up server software for automatically downloading files and then test and debug the system.
2. Purchase needed equipment.
3. Set up a training program for the sales force and prepare a new customer orientation training presentation.
4. Prepare new sales materials.
5. Run a 60-day beta test with three customers.

Detail the Advantages

We have looked at approaches to resolve the customer's problem of synchronizing files of people working on the road or at home. This is the only approach the IT department head feels will work. These are the main advantages of the strategy:

1. Strategy has been successfully implemented by others. Commercial software is available to expedite the introduction.

2. The service meets a key customer need that could become even more important as telecommuting becomes more popular.

3. We have the necessary skills and resources to implement the program.

4. The strategy has strong financials and exceeds the company's ROI requirements.

5. The program is a good start for creating recurring revenue streams from our customer base.

Ask for Action

We believe this strategy offers a strong new service that our customers want and that the strategy will provide the company strong sales and profit growth. We want to officially kick off this program June 1 with the hire of a new IT specialist and be ready for our customer introduction on December 1. I'm requesting approval from you today to move ahead. Are you prepared to give that approval now?

Presentation to Conservative Listeners— Address a New Opportunity

The Strategy

Post pages on social networking sites for the company's retail store products that will be managed by young retail associates. They will offer advice and answer questions about the store's electronic products and post notes about the "hot" new products or services in the store.

Craft the Opening Statement

The strategy I'll be presenting today is targeted at one of our important core markets, teenagers and young adults under 30 years old. This is a market where we need increased market share to grow in the future.

Show Careful Consideration

This important customer group increasingly gets their product and buying information over social networking sites like MySpace and Facebook. We need to respond to changing activities of our customer group or we risk being left behind. The rapid growth of the social networking sites has been well documented, and all studies reinforce that young people will continue increased use of these sites for product and buying information.

Introduce the Strategy (Background Statement Plus Statement of Strategy)

I'm concerned that the company may lose sales because of its lack of involvement in the social networking arena. The strategy I'm proposing is to set up social network pages on Facebook and MySpace named after the store, Barry's Electronic Network, and have 10 to 12 young sales associates create, maintain, and actively work the sites for each product category, which would include areas such as photography, games, and music downloads. The associates will post notes about new products, innovative ways to use products, tips for the best performance, and a sampling of customer comments we receive. The pages would be available across the country and team members would take turns responding to customer inquiries.

Address Listeners' Expected Concerns

I know this is a new direction for the company, and one that's new to most managers. But the young associates I've interviewed are all familiar with social network sites, and 90 percent of them have their own pages. The sites have an informal air to them, and if the sites don't work out we can close them. If we need to close the sites the damage to us will be minimal as the sites are informal, and our young associates will run the site with an informal air that minimizes the risk.

Show the Strategy as a Response

People under 30, and even many people over 30, visit the social networking sites every day and companies are starting to have pages that have an informal, low commercial tilt. We can't afford to just ignore this development as people are trading a great deal of product and store information on the sites. We need the right type of people running the sites. In this case we have the perfect people to run the program, our young retail associates who are a part of our target market.

Demonstrate a Good Fit

This is an important program because the target market is key to the company's growth. The associates I've spoken with feel they only need the standard images marketing has for their products already and they will be ready to go online once the strategy is approved. We also have a young product manager in marketing who understands the social networking sites and will lead the program. Our associates know their product area, understand the proper protocol to use, and are excited about moving forward.

Explain the Future Fit

This program is also important for the future of the company. The Internet era changes our marketing efforts on a regular basis. We can't wait to adapt to those changes until they are being written up in *Time* magazine. Our young team running the program will also be charged with keeping the company up to date on new developments so our Internet marketing programs can constantly evolve with our market.

Grow the Company

I believe we need this program to meet our per-store growth objectives. This target market represents 40 percent of our customer base and it accounts for 60 percent of our per-store sales growth over the last two years. We will start this program on a trial basis in one department, but when fully implemented we are projecting sales to this group to grow 10 percent per year.

Add Value to Customers

I believe, and the associates I spoke with feel, that the program has very high value to the customer group. Networking sites are very popular and many people spend over an hour or more per day on the sites. We will be offering information where our customer group likes to go. Plus customers will be able to get informal, though technically correct, answers to their questions. This program simply ties us into an extremely popular communication medium our customers are already using.

Detail the Costs

This is a low-cost program as we are currently using the software of the networking sites. We will start with just one product area, mp3 players. The cost of using the associates based on their usual pay rate will be $7,500 per month, and we will assign one young marketing person to lead the program. That person's payroll costs will be $6,500 per month. Other costs should run $2,000 to $3,000 per month. We eventually plan on having eight departments with social networking sites for a cost of approximately $35,000 per month.

Making Money

The potential financial rewards for this project are very high. Last year this target group purchased over $800 million in products from us. Even a 2 percent sales growth would produce an ROI of over 100 percent per year. We aren't positive what our actual sales growth will be from this program. That is why we are recommending today moving forward with the test in one product area.

Explain the Key Tasks

We have a straightforward plan for our test program with these tasks and assignments:

1. The marketing leader will prepare an introduction plan and select a team of associates to interact on the site.

2. The associates and marketing leader will determine all the materials they will need to execute the site and how they should be stored on the various social networking site servers.

3. The marketing leader will interface with an assigned person on the IT staff and the IT departments of the social networking sites to cover any issues that might arise.

4. A team of three associates and the marketing manager will set up guidelines for postings and responses. They will also set a monitoring schedule to be sure news is continuously updated.

5. The marketing team leader will coordinate schedules with the designated associates' retail managers to be sure they are available.

Detail the Advantages

From my conversations with others in the company there seems to be a consensus that we need to get our feet wet in this market arena. No one is sure what the results will be, but the feeling is we must learn more about how to handle these alternative media. These are the advantages of the proposal:

1. The proposal offers huge upside sales and profit potential with a key targeted customer group.

2. The strategy provides the company windows to new technologies and new methods of online communicating.

The company needs to be able to operate effectively as the Internet changes.

3. The company is able to capitalize on the savvy Internet skills of its young associates.

4. The program can be started as a test program to acquire more detailed data before launching a large-scale program.

Ask for Action

I believe we must pursue this program. We have little to lose with a test program, but we have a lot to lose if we ignore the new communications medium, especially one that is so important to a key core target customer. Today, I'd like to receive your approval to move ahead with the test program. I'd like to have it up and ready by the time the holiday season starts in three months. Do I have your approval to move ahead?

Chapter 16

Sample Presentations— Internal Strategies

Presentation to Management—Create a Competitive Advantage

The Strategy

For a sports stadium contractor: Develop commercially available software into a modeling package that will build a stadium project on a daily or weekly basis. The software will identify within two days when each step of work will occur. The benefit is that the contractor will be able to cost-effectively keep projects on time.

Craft the Opening Statement

The strategy I'm proposing today will allow us to be able to have the best on-time, on-budget record in the sports construction industry.

Show Careful Consideration

The strategy has an extremely visual component that will demonstrate how we can outperform the competition. That demonstration will enhance our image as the most progressive company in the industry. The strategy will also make the company's workforce more productive as they will spend their time actually building the project rather than chasing down materials and crew. We've been evaluating this strategy for two months and believe it represents a tremendous opportunity to the company.

Introduce the Strategy (Background Statement Plus Statement of Strategy)

We have six competitors in the sports stadium construction market, and the goal of every company is to have the best on-time, under-budget performance, a goal now missed by the industry on over 60 percent of ongoing projects. We have already implemented a software program with modeling capability to help us bid and build projects. I'm proposing that we take the modeling concept one step further and add the capability of building a project on the computer, step by step. That will allow us to know exactly what work will be done on a specific project every day. We will be able to better plan work staff and material purchases to keep costs down and projects on schedule.

Address Listeners' Expected Concerns

The cost savings of this project will be large. The commercial version of the software has been used on office buildings and it has cut 10 percent off the project time, has reduced breakage and scrap by 25 percent of material sitting in storage, and it has allowed companies to reduce their project management team by 15 percent. Best of all the companies are getting bonuses for finishing early and avoiding late penalties.

Show the Strategy as a Response

We are proposing this strategy because on every presentation, bid, and follow-up meeting the key question is always: can you finish on time. That's only natural as every project has a deadline. This project will allow us to meet the deadline up front with a better schedule based on a modeling program. This is far cheaper than the current method of pouring every available resource into the project hoping it comes in on time.

Demonstrate a Good Fit

We can execute this strategy now because our programming crew is available for a new project. The crew has finished and debugged the modeling software we have used for bidding projects over the last two years and has time for this new project. Two of the programmers have used the software package for other large projects in the past and they are confident that the software can be converted for our application. Outside of programming time, only about $45,000 of additional computer hardware and software is needed.

Explain the Future Fit

This project could play a major role in the company's long-term goal of increasing its market share from 14 to 20 percent. Cost and delivery are the two all-important variables for construction companies when they bid on a sports stadium project. This software will give us a major edge on our competitors in both categories.

Grow the Company

Our company is targeted to grow 15 percent per year over the next five years. This is an aggressive goal. We can only do that by providing better pricing and better delivery of our projects. This strategy helps the company deliver on both. We will cut our costs by having materials delivered when they will be needed, and by not having materials lying around that won't be required for several weeks. We will meet our delivery schedules by always being prepared for the next phase of the job.

Add Value to Customers

On-time, on-budget project completion is of course the number one customer concern. But this software gives an added value to customers. The software allows us to reprogram the construction model when customers request changes. We will be able to give more accurate timelines based on changes, and we will be able to make more changes without disrupting the promised delivery date.

Detail the Costs

The total cost of the project over the next two years will be $350,000. This includes $45,000 for computer software. We also are including the cost of our IT programmers. We won't have to hire new programmers for the software project, but we are counting their costs in the project as they may be laid off if we don't move ahead. We also expect to save anywhere from two to four people on the project management team with this software, but those savings are not included in the costs.

Making Money

The number one reason we are recommending moving forward on this project is that it will increase sales. But even without an increase, it will pay for itself three times over on just the first big project. We expect a minimum savings on a $250 million project of $1.2 million.

Explain the Key Tasks

Our IT programming leader will lead the project and is confident we can have it up and running in 15 months. These are the major tasks from the IT programming team's action item list:

1. Procure software license and develop the strategy's computer hardware requirements.
2. Create a detailed work plan for programmers to be ready for beta tests in 240 days.
3. Run a beta test on a past project, compare the results with actual project completion, and debug the program as needed.
4. Run the program on a smaller project after 12 months, debugging the program as needed.
5. In 15 months be prepared to run the next big project with the software modeling the actual construction process on a day-by-day basis.

Detail the Advantages

This strategy gives us a decided market advantage in major sports stadium construction that will lead to our winning a minimum of 10 percent more of the upcoming bids. These are the advantages that I believe are key to producing those sales results:

1. The software can be demonstrated during the bidding process, giving prospects confidence we will meet our cost and delivery dates.
2. The company will save time and costs completing the project, as much as 10 percent of our nonmaterial costs on any project.
3. We can quickly show the time and expense required on any customer-mandated changes.
4. We will know early when we are behind schedule and be able to take steps to get back on track.
5. We will minimize the chances of paying project late fees.

Ask for Action

This strategy provides a vehicle for the company to meet its market share, sales, and profit goals over the next three years and provides tremendous value to our customers. Today I'm requesting your approval to move forward with the project, procuring the software and starting the programming action plan and preliminary programming work. In 60 days we will offer an update report, verifying that our original projections are correct and then ask for approval to complete the project. Do we have your approval to move ahead with phase one? The cost for the first 60 days will be $30,000, which includes $5,000 for software and $25,000 of programming time.

Presentation to Action-Oriented People— Address a New Opportunity

The Strategy

Start using the TWI Productivity and Quality Efficiency Training Program for the company's line supervisors. The aim is to decrease substantially part-to-part variation in the company's products.

Craft the Opening Statement

I'm proposing today that we adopt a strategy that will quickly build momentum and morale of our shop floor line supervisors while at the same time improve our quality.

Show Careful Consideration

The training I'm proposing has been on the market for several years and has been adopted with great success by a number of companies around the country. The company offering the training has just opened up a local regional office. That office is staffed by people with extensive experience at the training company's East Coast offices.

Introduce the Strategy (Background Statement Plus Statement of Strategy)

I recommend the TWI Productivity and Quality Efficiency Training Program for the company because up until now we have not been able to pick up large orders from vehicle manufacturers. The main reason for our lack of success is that we have not shown that we can deliver products with a high level of consistent quality and because the vehicle manufacturers complain that we have too much part-to-part variation in our products. We can reserve every other Thursday for training for supervisors on production efficiency, and every Friday to teach employees how to effectively operate their equipment with the goal of reducing variation and fluctuations in our product quality.

Address Listeners' Expected Concerns

Plant management as well as the line supervisors support bringing in outside training as they have been frustrated in their efforts to bring the level of quality up to the vehicle manufacturers' standards. They understand that their lack of progress is a major impediment to the company's growth.

Show the Strategy as a Response

One of the reasons we want to move ahead quickly is that we are concerned our prospective vehicle customers will see us standing still. Bringing in a strong training team with an established reputation will allow marketing and sales to keep selling the fact the company is rapidly moving forward on this issue.

Demonstrate a Good Fit

Plant management and TWI will be ready to start the program 30 days after the strategy receives approval. TWI has worked with companies with similar technology in the past and plant management is confident that TWI is an excellent fit for our company.

Explain the Future Fit

This strategy plays a key role in our future. The company's growth plans include moving beyond our small- to mid-size customers to capture some of the major vehicle manufacturing accounts. In order to do that, we need a high quality level with at least six sigma quality and preferably twelve sigma. This training plays an important role in meeting that goal.

Grow the Company

Landing a large account will increase our business 50 percent and provide the justification we need to expand our plant 75 percent, and modernize our equipment to increase productivity. If we aren't able to expand, we won't meet the company's goals for 60 percent sales growth with a 20 percent decrease in costs over the next three years. If we wait too long to upgrade, other companies will step in this window of opportunity to land large vehicle accounts and then those companies will be difficult to dislodge.

Add Value to Customers

Our current customers will also be happy to see these improvements. It will cut their incoming quality inspection time. They will also have an easier time keeping or acquiring their quality certifications if our products ship with a guarantee that states our products meet or exceed either six or twelve sigma standards.

Detail the Costs

The TWI training cost of this 12-month program will be $600,000. This cost includes initial training, and then follow-up with participants on their work plans and goals for each station, and finally follow-up in the final three months. We will also have a cost of $175,000 throughout the program for quality testing to monitor by station our product deviations.

Making Money

This program will have a return if we land one of the large vehicle accounts. The smallest of the four potential accounts would have sales of $4 million per year, with a 15 percent profit or $600,000. If we land that account our payback would be in 15 months and we would have an annual ROI of 77.4 percent. The largest account has sales of $11.5 million and if we landed that account our payoff period would be less than six months and our ROI per year would be 220 percent. The financials are strong and we and TWI are both ready to move forward 30 days after the project is approved.

Explain the Key Tasks

The plant is ready to move on the project and execute this timeline:

1. Sign the agreement with TWI.

2. Conduct a three-month program of initial training of the line supervisors in the plant.

3. Prepare a station evaluation outlining key performance items, work plan, and in-process test reports. Additional test reports will be provided upon completion as well. This phase will take three months and TWI will provide assistance on these projects once a week.

4. Evaluate the per-station test results, modify work plan and tests as needed to ensure the process is working correctly at each station. This phase will also take three months.

5. Evaluate final product consistency, determine sigma level, determine what areas if any are creating deficiencies in product consistency, put in required controls, and make adjustments as needed. This final phase is three months and at the conclusion we should be operating at or beyond our six sigma quality target.

Detail the Advantages

We don't anticipate any problems putting this strategy into action. TWI has done a thorough review of our operations and our production methods are close to three other companies the local team has worked on in the past. The advantages of the program are significant:

1. We will substantially increase our odds of landing the big vehicle account we need to achieve our growth goals.

2. We will have a strong quality program that will allow us to start the process of obtaining our own quality certifications.

3. The strategy should cut our scrap rate and improve our productivity at each station.

4. The training of the line supervisors in how to approach and solve problems will be beneficial as the company continues to work on improving its productivity and quality.

Ask for Action

One reason I am strongly recommending this strategy is because the entire training process has been motivational for both plant management and line supervisors in other companies. For us, this increased motivation should carry forth to all aspects of the plant, which will provide a boost in the company's performance. Today I would like to receive approval to set up a demonstration of the TWI process that can be given in the next two weeks to management. I believe management will want to move forward after seeing the results TWI has been able to achieve in the past. I'd like to set the date in two weeks on the 23rd. Do you want me to move ahead to set up this presentation?

Presentation to Analytical People— Solve a Problem

The Strategy

The company involved runs events from large banquets to conventions and primarily uses independent contractors who work on average 15 to 30 hours per month for the company. They also work other part-time jobs and the company has trouble scheduling people efficiently, periodically scheduling people to be in two places at once or not scheduling enough people for an event. The strategy is to replace its current scheduling system with an improved scheduling software system.

Craft the Opening Statement

I'm proposing a strategy that is designed to finely tune the number of workers at each of our events so we can both cut internal costs and improve our service levels. The benefits of the program are strong and they significantly outweigh the costs.

Show Careful Consideration

This strategy I'm proposing has been used by several companies similar to ours in other parts of the country. They have been able to cut office staff and reduce their number of events with either too few or too many workers by 60 percent. The strategy has a modest cost up front in software and training but offers in return strong benefits to the company.

Introduce the Strategy (Background Statement Plus Statement of Strategy)

We currently have between 30 to 200 on call workers at big events at the convention center. When multiple events are running, scheduling those workers is a problem, as we don't have a good method of tracking people and knowing where or when they are committed to work for us, or when they are available to work. As a result, we may over-schedule people for an event, hoping to get the right number, but often we end up with too many or too few workers at an event. At the last Industry Convention a new software staffing program was developed that coordinated available people with the events being run. The program sent e-mails to contractors with their weekly assignments that they can either accept or reject and automatically replaces contractors who are not available with an alternate. I recommend we purchase this software to improve the use of our on-call staff at our customer training events.

Address Listeners' Expected Concerns

We have experienced the problem of the right staffing levels repeatedly over the last three years and have added office staff to call people, check on availability, and finalize schedules. But frequently they can't get in touch with people. As a result we have higher office costs without solving the problem. We've reviewed many solutions and are confident this software package is by far our best option.

Show the Strategy as a Response

Clearly we have a problem in scheduling, which is a major reason the company is only bidding on 18 percent of the quote requests it receives. Another reason we need to move ahead, even if we choose not to grow, is the high costs associated with our current attempts at solving the problem. We have three extra people in the office, and we estimate we average 5 percent extra people on major events in order to be sure we have sufficient coverage.

Demonstrate a Good Fit

We currently outsource our IT work, and the high hourly cost is one reason we have chosen the solutions we've used before.

Now we have been able to negotiate with our IT provider for better terms and the provider has agreed to give us a fixed cost for setting up the software and a standard monthly fee for operating the system on an ongoing basis. The firm has reviewed the software and talked both to the provider and current users and is confident it can install and debug the software in 60 days.

Explain the Future Fit

To date, our scheduling problems have prevented the company from tackling large-scale events with many smaller events occurring at the same time. The company has also limited the number of events it will run at any given time. This software package will remove those constraints.

Grow the Company

The company would like to bid on many more projects, as well as bid on the large events that occur in this market two to three times per year. That is the only way the company can increase its growth rate from 3 percent per year to management's goal of 15 percent year. Other companies that have used this system have grown over 20 percent per year, and they have started to bid on every event where they project a profit margin of over 30 percent.

Add Value to Customers

This strategy also provides a significant value to customers and event planners. They want every project to go smoothly without any conflicts or problems at a reasonable price. We should be able to reduce or hold prices once we adopt this strategy. We will also be sure not to be short-staffed at any event. This is a serious concern as our customer surveys showed 22 percent of the respondents were concerned that we did not have enough staff present for their event.

Detail the Costs

The software package will be $17,500, the installation costs from our IT provider will be $22,500, and their ongoing monthly charges for maintenance, debugging, and support will be $5,000. We will recover the costs with internal savings and none of these costs will be passed on to the customer.

Making Money

The program will pay for itself in the first year even if we don't increase business because we will be able to reduce our scheduling staff. Our accountant's evaluation shows we have a nine-month payback period and an ongoing ROI of 125 percent without a sales increase. If we increase sales 20 percent as expected in the second year, our ROI will be over 300 percent. This is by far the best solution to the problem and also a much higher return than the company has ever gotten before implementing new technology.

Explain the Key Tasks

The implementation of this project will be undertaken by our IT provider and the Project Manager who handles the scheduling of contractors. The IT provider has worked out these key tasks based on implementing the plan in July and August when our activity levels are low:

1. Purchase software and attend a one-week training course at the software provider's location.
2. Use three IT provider staffers for one month to complete installation and training of company staff.
3. Use one IT staffer to run three test cycles and debug the program as needed.
4. Use the software for the first time at the end of August for the Thrivant Financial Midwest Region conference.

Detail the Advantages

This software package has been evaluated by our IT provider as well as several other companies. It is a clear winner in its benefits-to-costs ratio against both nonsoftware solutions and other software solutions. It provides the following strong advantages for the company:

1. Offers the company a window to growth it hasn't been able to pursue in the past.
2. Cuts office staff which can't be flexed up and down as needed.
3. Minimizes the cost of having too many contractors present to work at an event.
4. Minimizes complaints from customers that the company didn't have enough workers present.

Ask for Action

I believe strongly that this solution is the best option for the company—it doesn't just solve the problem; it allows the company to grow in the future. The costs are reasonable, the returns are high, and customers will be better served. To implement this program in the slow summer months I need your approval to move ahead starting June 1. To start on that date I'd like your approval to move forward. Do you feel comfortable approving the strategy today?

Presentation to Conservative Listeners— Improve Performance

The Strategy

The company is a new Internet company that has been funded by sophisticated investors. The strategy explored is preparing standard work statements for each position in the company to clarify which person has responsibility and accountability for each task.

Craft the Opening Statement

I'm proposing a strategy today that I believe will help our company grow with orderly, efficient growth. I feel without efficiency, our desired growth rate is not obtainable.

Show Careful Consideration

I've tracked other high-growth Internet companies over the last three years, and found that only 30 percent could sustain their initial high growth, and a significant percentage of them imploded. The successful ones moved beyond "the kids in the dorm room" management style to a more efficient method of getting the work done.

Introduce the Strategy (Background Statement Plus Statement of Strategy)

As we have expanded rapidly we have been hiring people to fill in the gaps and get the work out but we have evolved to a helter-skelter approach where everyone attacks the most pressing issue. I'm proposing we implement a new strategy where we adopt the Lean Management approach of having a standard work statement for each employee. This will help us ensure that every task is addressed in a timely manner, and that there is a person responsible and accountable for each task in the company.

Address Listeners' Expected Concerns

I realize it is not easy to propose a change when the company is flying high. But I feel strongly that now is the time to change, before we increase our staffing again and the situation becomes out of control. We need to heed the lessons of other Internet companies.

Show the Strategy as a Response

I'm proposing this strategy as a response to two recent problems where we failed to deliver for a customer because everyone was attending to what was considered to be a pressing problem. I know people feel that they just have to be more careful in the future, and we can do that with 10 to 12 employees. But now we have expanded to 20, and soon we will have 50 employees and we can't count on people just being more observant to catch every task that is slipping through the cracks.

Demonstrate a Good Fit

Two of our current employees come from successful companies that had added structure, responsibilities, and accountability to their organization. Right now they are in a loose way trying to organize the company, but they do face some resistance. We can incorporate their organizational experience and have them lead our team that will introduce work statements. The initial phase of this process will take less than 30 days at our current staffing level. As we add more employees the organization may be too unwieldy to easily introduce this strategy.

Explain the Future Fit

I understand of course that this strategy will disrupt the organization on a short-term basis and many employees like the current free-flowing situation where everyone operates as equals. But that is not the right approach for the future. I believe we can all see that clearly our organization won't work with 50 to 100 employees the same way it can work with 12. We need to change now, even though it may be uncomfortable, if we are to grow in the future.

Grow the Company

Growth is the key word to this strategy because the company has taken on large investors who want the company ready to offer public stock in 24 months. That calls for an aggressive growth plan over the next two years. That growth will require new organizational skills. Lean Management is a well-accepted strategy, adopted by many companies as the preferred approach. There are many consultants we can utilize to help our team members put this strategy in place initially, and to help with its continued implementation as the company grows.

Add Value to Customers

I believe these changes are essential to meet our customers' needs. We are not just selling a ready-to-go solution for every customer. We are selling a solution that needs to be customized for each customer. Customers want projects delivered on time and on budget, and they want to feel they have complete access to our company. That includes every customer, small and large. We can provide and will provide that service if we change over now to a work statement approach.

Detail the Costs

Right now we can implement this strategy with a team of our two employees with experience in companies with organizations similar to what we are proposing, and by hiring a Lean Management consulting firm to assist us. The initial costs, including our employees working one-third of the time on the project, will be $15,000 per month. We expect costs of $15,000 for the first 12 months until department managers have enough Lean Management experience to maintain the work statements in their departments. Our costs will be much higher if we wait until our organization grows to the point where it can't operate effectively before trying to reorganize.

Making Money

Besides offering the only way to grow effectively, the Lean Management system promised tremendous financial returns. Lean Management has documented savings as much as 20 percent in employee costs for similar productivity, has helped companies grow profitability while constantly increasing per-employee productivity, and has cut the annual costs of correcting mistakes by 25 percent.

Explain the Key Tasks

We have identified two employees with a suitable background to lead the internal implementation team. The Lean Management system has been utilized successfully in enough applications that we can be confident it will succeed, and I don't foresee anyone proposing alternatives or offering strong resistance to the plans. These are the key tasks we will undertake if the strategy is approved and a consultant is hired:

1. Produce a complete list of key tasks that must be performed for the company to succeed.
2. Assign preliminary people to the tasks based in part on the work tasks they routinely take on as a leader and assign staff to each leader.
3. Review assignments with management for approval, make adjustments as needed.
4. Review proposed assignments given to staff leaders, adjustments made as needed.
5. Conduct separate training for leaders and staff.

6. Leaders and staff will work with the lead team and consultant to develop work statements, responsibilities, and accountability for each employee.

Detail the Advantages

We believe this strategy will have strong support within the company. The strategy has been proven in many areas of business. Already people perceive our organizational structure is reaching the end of its usefulness as we grow, and the program has strong financial benefits. These are the other advantages:

1. We have 2 out of 20 employees who have experience with the proposed changes and who will take a lead role in a fast implementation program.
2. Investors will be pleased we are making a major change in the operations of the organization to position the company for rapid future growth.
3. Our company is at a size where we can implement these changes without any disruption to our normal operations.
4. We will be adopting a strategy where there is a wealth of experience at other companies, and a wide variety of experts to guide the company through a successful implementation.

Ask for Action

I believe the company can't continue to grow and prosper unless we change our organization so it can continue to be efficient as we grow rapidly. I also believe that it will be a mistake waiting until the organization becomes dysfunctional to change. That will damage our image in the market and with our investors. Waiting will also make implementing the strategy more difficult and expensive. I am requesting today that you approve the strategy of implementing work statements for each employee with a start date for implementation of October 1. Are you ready to authorize the company to move forward on this plan?

About the Author

Don Debelak has over 30 years experience primarily in business development and marketing both as a consultant and as an employee of companies of all sizes and in positions from entry level sales to president. He has made numerous business strategy presentations to companies in all stages of development from start-ups to companies with over 100 years of history. Debelak has successfully presented and prepared numerous strategies over his career from improving an invoice format to changing the target customer and modifying the main product line of a million dollar corporation

Don Debelak was the columnist of Bright Ideas for *Entrepreneur* magazine from 1999 to 2005 and is the author of 14 business books including *Perfect Phrases for Business Meetings* (McGraw-Hill, 2008), *Perfect Phrases for Business Proposals and Plans* (McGraw-Hill, 2005), and *Business Models Made Easy* (Entrepreneur Media, 2006). He has been interviewed on national radio shows and Internet business shows and has been featured in leading magazines including the *Wall Street Journal* and *Washington Post*. He is currently president of Liqtech NA, a manufacturer of diesel particulate filters for heavy duty trucks, a business he developed in North America after presenting a strategy to the Denmark company who owned the technology.

The Right Phrase for Every Situation...Every Time.

Perfect Phrases for Building Strong Teams
Perfect Phrases for Business Letters
Perfect Phrases for Business Proposals and Business Plans
Perfect Phrases for Business School Acceptance
Perfect Phrases for College Application Essays
Perfect Phrases for Cover Letters
Perfect Phrases for Customer Service
Perfect Phrases for Dealing with Difficult People
Perfect Phrases for Dealing with Difficult Situations at Work
Perfect Phrases for Documenting Employee Performance Problems
Perfect Phrases for Executive Presentations
Perfect Phrases for Landlords and Property Managers
Perfect Phrases for Law School Acceptance
Perfect Phrases for Lead Generation
Perfect Phrases for Managers and Supervisors
Perfect Phrases for Medical School Acceptance
Perfect Phrases for Meetings
Perfect Phrases for Motivating and Rewarding Employees
Perfect Phrases for Negotiating Salary & Job Offers
Perfect Phrases for Perfect Hiring
Perfect Phrases for the Perfect Interview
Perfect Phrases for Performance Reviews
Perfect Phrases for Real Estate Agents & Brokers
Perfect Phrases for Resumes
Perfect Phrases for Sales and Marketing Copy
Perfect Phrases for the Sales Call
Perfect Phrases for Setting Performance Goals
Perfect Phrases for Small Business Owners
Perfect Phrases for the TOEFL Speaking and Writing Sections
Perfect Phrases for Writing Grant Proposals
Perfect Phrases in American Sign Language for Beginners
Perfect Phrases in French for Confident Travel
Perfect Phrases in German for Confident Travel
Perfect Phrases in Italian for Confident Travel
Perfect Phrases in Mexican Spanish for Confident Travel
Perfect Phrases in Spanish for Construction
Perfect Phrases in Spanish for Gardening and Landscaping
Perfect Phrases in Spanish for Household Maintenance and Childcare
Perfect Phrases in Spanish for Restaurant and Hotel Industries

Visit mhprofessional.com/perfectphrases for a complete product listing.

Learn more. Do more.